Arkansas
OFF THE BEATEN PATH

Arkansas

OFF THE
BEATEN
PATH™

PATTI DeLANO

A Voyager Book

The Globe Pequot Press

Old Saybrook, Connecticut

Text illustrations by Cathy Johnson
Cover map © DeLorme Mapping

Library of Congress Cataloging-in Publication Data

Delano, Patti
  Arkansas—off the beaten path / by Patti DeLano.—1st ed.
    p. cm.
  "A Voyager book"
  Includes index.
  ISBN 1-56440-013-1
  1. Arkansas—Guidebooks. I. Title.
F409.3.D45   1992
917.6704'53–dc20   92-12549
                                                             CIP

Manufactured in the United States of America
First Edition/Second Printing

To Bob and Chris,
who encouraged me on my first solo,
and to Cathy, who dared me to do it

ARKANSAS

Contents

Acknowledgments

Finding offbeat places in Arkansas often means following directions like "You know where that big ole tree used to be? Hang a left there you know, by that red barn?"

So I owe a lot to Tyler Hardeman and Carol VanPelt at the Department of Parks and Tourism for providing suggestions and some of the photographs for the artwork. I especially thank Art and Terry Hapke, who offered hospitality and help from their home in Fairfield Bay and spent endless hours helping me find places as common as antiques shops and as remote as an elephant farm. My mom and dad, Sally and John Randazzo, also endured mountain roads and odd places, with the sense of humor I love them for, as we wandered around the state. And, of course, I thank my husband, Bob, who has an instinct for finding unique eating places (he keeps promising a mystery restaurant called the "Blue Goofus" that's just over the hill, when I am so hungry that road-kill is beginning to look good) and unlikely shortcuts not shown on any map (even if he's never been there before)—making travel with him fun, and my books a lot more interesting.

Introduction

Arkansas is the perfect vacationland: 60-foot waterfalls and quiet sandbars seen only from a canoe or wooded hiking trail. Add trout streams and hunting lodges—nature at its best for people who want to be outdoors—plus golf courses, racetracks, and the big-city fun of fine restaurants, and you have the vacation choice of millions in the nation's heartland.

Thousands of artists and craftspeople have settled in the Ozarks. Vineyards and wineries dot the Arkansas River Valley, and an elephant breeding farm lies hidden in the foothills. You will find the friendliness of the Old South, hardy spirit of the Southwest, and practicality of the Midwest in the people here.

This undiscovered wonderland, far from any ocean, may be one of the most beautiful states on the continent. It has more designated national Scenic Byways than any other in the nation. But Arkansas is more than just the beauty of stair-step waterfalls or Class V rapids in a canoe. It offers wine country, good Cajun food, old cotton plantations, and the only bordello on the National Register of Historic Places. If that's too much excitement for you, there's a Benedictine monastery where you can retreat, search your soul, and start over.

The climate boasts four distinct seasons—but with Gulf air creating the moderate temperatures of the southern United States. Spring comes early, attracting visitors from bordering states not so lucky in the weather game. Unlike its northern neighbors, Arkansas has a long, long spring filled with pleasant days perfect for outdoor activities.

Golfers, fishermen, hikers, and canoeists flock here. So do people who have retired from the rat race and do all their racing now on white-water rapids or at the greyhound or horse track. Arkansans are serious about outdoor activities. No wimps can be found on the 225-mile Ouachita Trail, which allows hikers to follow the ridges and valleys from Pinnacle Mountain State Park to Queen Wilhelmina State Lodge and into Oklahoma.

Yes, it's hot as the dickens in August, but as the muscadine grapes (known as scuppernongs) ripen to a reddish brown, the nights begin to cool. In late September the blackgum trees change from glossy green to shining crimson—suddenly and completely—standing out from the green of the other, more hesitant trees. Then other colors begin as casual blushes of yellow

Introduction

and red and spread from north to south during October to finish in a blaze of color. Fall colors are dazzling, and the endless days of perfect weather and bright blue skies make this about the best time of year.

Winters are characterized by brief cold snaps and a splash of clean snow, with crisp nights, bright stars, and crystal ice formations in the gleaming winter sun—followed quickly by warmer days. Mistletoe and five kinds of holly grow throughout the state, making hunting in the December woods popular.

The name Arkansas means "South Wind," the name of the Quapaw Indian tribe the French Jesuits met. It was written in their journals as it sounded and ended up as Arkansas. The state instrument is, of course, the fiddle—with free folk music concerts on town squares across the state. The state gem is the diamond, because Arkansas has the only diamond mine in the country and it's open for public digging! The state bird is the mockingbird, and that bird of many beautiful songs reflects this state's charming ambience and why people bent on having a bit of everything are drawn to this natural wonderland.

Because this book is filled with listings of small crafts shops, mom-and-pop restaurants, bed-and-breakfasts in beautiful old homes, and log cabins tucked in sleepy "hollers" and mountain foothills, it is wise to call ahead and double-check before making a long drive to a particular place. When something disappears, something else pops up in its place; getting off the beaten path in this state is always interesting. If something is gone or some other fascinating place has sprung up, let the publisher know about it so we can include it in the next update of this book.

The tourist information centers will give you a free road map, or you can call 1–800–NATURAL and get a vacation guide for the area you are visiting. Bring your camera or your sketch pad and find the best Mother Nature has to offer. That's why they call it the Natural State.

Off the Beaten Path in Northeast Arkansas

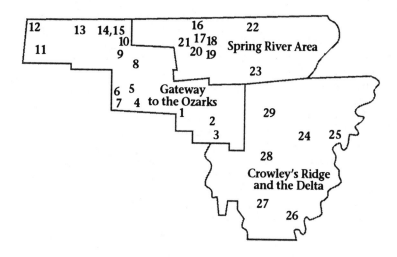

1. Arkansaw Traveller Gourmet Foods
2. *Mary Woods Number 2* steamboat
3. Pearls Unique
4. Mountain View
5. Ozark Folk Center
6. Ozark Mountain Trail Rides
7. Meadowcreek Environmental Center
8. River View Hotel
9. Wolf House
10. P.J.'s Lodge
11. Mountain Pines Cabin
12. Aunt Shirley's Sleeping Loft Bed and Breakfast
13. Concert Vineyards Winery
14. Country Reflections
15. Country Cottage Tea Room
16. Roseland Inn
17. Old Stone House Bed and Breakfast
18. Flat Creek Dulcimer Shop
19. Hardy Pottery
20. Naturals
21. Arkansas Indian Culture Center and Folklore Museum
22. Maynard Pioneer Museum
23. Reed's Wheatweavings
24. Museum Lepanto, USA
25. Hampson Museum State Park
26. Snowden House Plantation Bed and Breakfast Resort
27. Clint's
28. Granpa's Bargain Barn
29. Piero & Company Ristorante

Northeast Arkansas

Things don't change much in the Ozarks—dogwoods, redbuds, and wild plum bloom in the spring; wildflowers color the meadows of summer; and thousands of acres of autumn forest splash color over the hills where the clear-running streams and rivers still sparkle in the sun. The colors of the Ozarks shift like a kaleidoscope, but things in the Ozarks don't change much.

The pace is slower here. The people are friendly. In a place that did not have a paved highway until after the Second World War, a culture emerged unique in the country. In fact many people here insist that the Ozarks should have been its own state instead of meandering across two state lines.

Four beautifully different seasons bring vacationers to the Ozarks year-round. Hikers follow trails up grades to towering bluffs that cast soft shadows on the waters and offer views of pristine valleys. Gentle wildlife hide in the forest, and the scenes change with light and shadow.

These gentle, timeworn hills roll across the horizon without jagged peaks or sharp edges. A palette of colors—pale pink anemone in the early spring, soft shades of green in summer, blazing gold and crimson in fall, gray-green rock faces and clean white snow in winter—splash the canvas of cobalt blue sky.

Spring slips into the state early—while snow still clings to the rest of the heartland—and woods burst with the glory of dogwoods, redbuds, jonquils, sarvis, and wild azaleas before summer's rich green canopy shades the trails of the quiet foothills.

Bed-and-breakfast inns are not too common in Arkansas, and many of them are hidden in the woods. They are all worth searching out, so many of them are included here. Arkansas and Ozarks Bed and Breakfast is a referral service for a number of the B & Bs. Call Caroline Eck at (501) 297–8764 or 297–8211.

Gateway to the Ozarks

Batesville calls itself the "Gateway to the Ozarks"; it is a logical place to start. The town was founded in 1822 where the Southwest Trail met the White River crossing. (Some folks decided not to cross and stayed.) It is now the home of Arkansas College, and there is always something interesting going on in this college town. The annual Ozark Scottish Festival, held in the spring, features competitions in bagpiping, drumming, dancing, and athletics at the college campus, and the Batesville Air Festival, held each autumn, has thirty hot-air balloons in the air daily, along with antique and rare aircraft. If you have a sweet tooth, head downtown to the **Arkansaw Traveller Gourmet Foods.** In this little storefront shop, you can watch Donice and Charles Woodward make molded chocolate candies—offered in white, dark, and diet chocolate—as well as jam, jelly, butters, popcorn, and peanut or pecan brittle, all made in the shop and all available to taste. The shop is located at 600 Harrison Street; call (501) 793–7936.

From Batesville the White River flows southeast to the town of Jacksonport. Jacksonport State Park and Museum, 3 miles north on Highway 69, is the permanent home of *Mary Woods Number 2,* a refurbished, upriver packet stern-wheeler moored at the park; it's authentically outfitted with furnishings typical of the late 1800s, the heyday of the steamboat era. With speeds up to 20 miles per hour, the steamer braved snags, sandbars, shoals, and boiler explosions; life expectancy of a riverboat was only about five years. More than 117 steamers were lost on the Arkansas River before 1872, and the White River offered some of the greatest challenges for riverboat crews. But the smaller packet steamers could move in only 3 feet of water and would venture up the smaller rivers, at least during the rainy season.

Its present location is a just resting place for the old steamer, because Jacksonport refused right-of-way to the railroad in 1872. A riverboat town to the end, Jacksonport was bypassed by the railroads and began to decline in the 1870s; in 1891 the county seat was moved, and the stores, saloons, and wharves disappeared. Admission for the museum is $1.50 for adults and 75 cents for children; call (501) 523–2143.

Highway 67 follows the White River south to Newport, where since the turn of the century both the White and the Black rivers that converge near Newport have yielded delicately tinted natural pearls that are highly valued, becoming heirlooms for families lucky enough to find them. In fact the Royal Crown of England has a lustrous White River pearl in it, and Richard Burton bought one valued at $37,000 for Elizabeth Taylor in 1969.

Pearls Unique is the place to find these rare beauties. The freshwater pearls are found in mussels in the cold river waters and, because of channeling, dredging, and pollution, are becom-

Mary Woods Number 2

ing rare. They come in all sizes, from the tiny ones to large collectors' pearls, and range in price from $5.00 to $20,000.00. The pearls are not just round; they come in shapes carrying such romantic names as angel wings, rosebud, snail, and popcorn. Customers have the option of selecting from loose pearls and having a setting custom-designed or finding a piece already made. Managers Phyllis Holmes and Jan Pratt Sink will explain how the value of the pearls is determined—by size, luster, shape, and color. Colors can be in shades of peach, apricot, rose, lavender, bronze, silver, gold, cream, white, or even blue and green. The shop has some very rare collectors' baroques, including a large white snail shape. Pearls Unique is located at 1902-D McLain, in Pratt Square. Hours are from about 8:00 A.M. to 4:30 P.M., but call ahead to make an appointment: (501) 523–3639 or (800) 637–3233.

Travel northeast from Newport on Highway 14 as it flows along the curve of the White River; the scene changes as mountains begin to pop up, trees begin to line the highway, and cattle graze on the rolling hills and valleys. The drive to Mountain View is an event in itself. You can take Highway 14 to Mountain View (cross the White River on the free ferry at Guion from 6:30 A.M. to 6:30 P.M.; then take the gravel road to Highway 14) or, for a drive through some lovely Ozark countryside, travel north on Highway 69 and then east on Highway 58. You can also stay on Highway 69, turning east on Highway 9, a twisting two-laner from Melbourne along a ridge with a view of White River Valley. No matter how you do it, the last 30 miles scribble through the hills with rocky streams and spectacular vistas. All roads lead to Mountain View, so it becomes the center point from which directions to other attractions in the area begin.

Free Saturday musicals held in the **Mountain View** town square have been a tradition for some thirty years, and "pickin' and grinnin'" goes on well into the night as local strummers gather by the courthouse and folks bring lawn chairs to get comfortable on balmy evenings. Folk music lovers by the thousands come into town to hear the fiddles and dulcimers sing. Favorite son Dick Powell, crooner and leading man of the forties and fifties, was born here. Mountain View also has the annual Bean Fest. More than thirty huge iron kettles of pinto beans, along with cornbread and onions, are cooked and served free to everyone. The tall-tale-telling contest (and they get taller every year) is part of the event called "The Big Blowout." But the highlight is the Great Outhouse Race—each privy is decorated and, after the musket shot, pushed along the course with the driver sitting on the seat inside. The coveted gold, silver, or bronze toilet seat trophies and cash prizes for best-decorated comfort station and most well-dressed driver are awarded on the courthouse steps. This is not the only outhouse race in the state, but it is, citizens here will tell you, the only one fueled by beans.

Courthouse Square is the heart of the community, and most of the shops have no address; in fact there are only a few street names. Highways become streets, streets become highways, and the names are interchangeable. Ask directions and the people who live in Mountain View will just point, or say it's near some other place on the square. If you walk around the square, you will find everything sooner or later. A number of B & Bs are clustered near the square. Commercial Hotel, on the northeast corner of the square across from the old jailhouse, is owned by Todd and Andrea Budy and calls itself a "vintage guest house." This B & B, located at the corner of Peabody and Washington streets, has eight rooms (three with private baths), the prices ranging from $33 to $69; call (501) 269–4383 for reservations. Popular with the local residents is the Hearthstone Bakery on the first floor of the hotel. It's run by Michael Warshauer and full of wickedly delicious treats and healthy lunches (the cream of peanut soup is most unusual, with its delicate trace of peanut flavor in a thick cream soup); call (501) 269–3297.

Peabody Street crosses Main at the south end of the square, and just past the post office is where Owl Hollow Country Inn Bed and Breakfast sits in the shade of old maple trees. Many of the musicians you will hear on the square stay here. It was built in the early 1900s. Maple trees surround the second-story porch where people pick and play well into the night when the weather is warm. Barbara and Doug Mitchell and Marilyn and George Ivy are owners. "People like it simple and plain like it used to be," says Barbara. Since the inn is only steps away from Courthouse Square where good musicmaking and jiggin' can be enjoyed almost every night, it is often booked up. Bring your fiddle and join in. Call Barbara or Marilyn at (501) 269–8699. Rooms at the inn—located at 219 South Peabody on Highway 9 South—are $40 and up, some with private baths. An old-fashioned breakfast is served at 8:00 A.M.

The Ironworks is a historic building on Courthouse Square. It has a complete line of hand-forged iron from the Stone County Ironworks, as well as an ice cream parlor and sweetshop. During the season, April through October, buggy rides around town originate here. (Buggy rides are $3.00 for adults and $2.00 for children.) Manager Lenore Shouts has recently opened the upstairs with more crafts, decorative accessories, and goodies of all kinds. Hours are seasonal and different almost every day: Opening at

9:00 A.M. daily, the shop stays open until 5:00, 6:00, and 7:00 P.M. on weeknights and until 9:00 and 10:00 P.M. on weekends. Winter hours are Tuesday through Saturday from 9:00 A.M. to 5:00 P.M.; call (501) 269–3999 for the exact closing time.

The Inn at Mountain View just off the courthouse square at 307 Washington, dates to 1886 and features a porch that is great for sitting and rocking. A large stone fireplace in the living room warms guests on cool autumn nights. Owners Bob and Jenny Williams are no ordinary innkeepers. Jenny has filled the inn with antiques, handmade quilts, and fresh flowers. At 8:30 A.M., Bob is the breakfast chef, whipping up Belgian waffles, raspberry ambrosia, or his own biscuits and sausage gravy while telling tall tales to guests around the kitchen table. Telephones and television are not available, but the restored inn is air conditioned. Large mini-suites range in price from $52 to $88 and all have private baths. Call (800) 535–1301 or (501) 269–4200 for reservations.

The Ozark Artisans Mall is a half-block east of Courthouse Square on Main Street. Owners Linda and Charles Widmer show the wares of some eighty area craftspeople. The Widmers are wood-carvers, creating everything from little animals at $20 to life-size figures for much, much more. The *Mountain Man and Dog*, for example, carved from sassafras wood, is $12,000. Optimus Art Company is there, too, where silversmith John Pool designs unique silver jewelry. There are also shops specializing in pottery, wood-carvings, custom furniture, and tole paintings. The mall is open Monday through Saturday from 9:00 A.M. to 5:30 P.M. Call (501) 269–4774 for more information.

Also east of the square but on Sylamore Road (which is also Highway 9) is where Lynn McSpadden and his team of craftpeople make dulcimers at McSpadden's Dulcimer Shop. The shop is filled with local artists' crafts—pottery, wood-carvings—all natural items. You can watch through the glass wall as five woodworkers make Mountain Dulcimers (that's the kind that go on your lap). If you ask, someone will play one and give you a quick lesson. They'll have you playing "Mary Had a Little Lamb" in no time. Prices here are quite reasonable—from $180 with a case, music, and instructions to $1,000 for a custom-carved beauty. The shop is open from April through October; call (501) 269–4313.

Main Street becomes Highway 5/9/14 a few blocks east of the square. Turn north at the intersection and you will find the Arkansas Craft Guild shop, the showcase for the best artists from all over the state. Linda VonTrump, executive director, says that more than 300 artists are members of the guild, and they have been sending top-quality, handmade crafts here for more than twenty years. Several guild shops dot the state. This one is open from 9:30 A.M. to 5:00 P.M. every day except Sunday from April through January. Call Linda at (501) 269–3897.

Two miles north of Mountain View on Highway 5/9/14 is the Jimmy Driftwood Barn. If you don't know who Jimmy Driftwood is, you will know by the time you leave Mountain View. The Jimmy Driftwood Barn was built by him for the Rackensack Folk-lore Society, a loose-knit group of locals who are dedicated to pre-serving the folk music of the hills. It is operated by the University of Central Arkansas. Driftwood has been called this country's finest folk balladeer, although he started his career quite by acci-dent at age fifty, when he wrote "The Battle of New Orleans" for his sixth-grade American history class and it became an instant success. The barn welcomes folk musicians and the public to free Friday musicals throughout the year.

What brings people to the Mountain View area, though, is the **Ozark Folk Center,** north of town off Highway 5/9/14 on Folk Center Road. Built to maintain the unique folk traditions of the Ozarks, the center preserves almost-forgotten arts and music of the hill people who lived on the hillsides and "hollers" of the mountains. Artists like Dutch Wigman, who makes bowed psalteries; Terri Bruhin, a weaver who makes lace-weave table linens and rag rugs (more about her later); and Owen Rein, a mas-ter chairmaker who creates white oak rockers with drawknife and bending forms, or "jigs," to curve the green wood to the measure-ments of the person planning to use it, show their skills at the center. This showcase for hill-life traditions was founded by descendants of the river valley pioneers to preserve the lore and crafts that were quickly disappearing. Twenty-five "cabin crafts," practiced in rustic shops scattered across an Ozark hilltop, and a heritage herb garden are open daily from 10:00 A.M. to 5:00 P.M. The park renews a time when simple materials like white oak sheaves or apples became baskets and dolls and when common farm implements like sawblades and buckets became musical instruments. Music is made here with such instruments as the bowed psaltry, dulcimer, pickin' bow, and spoons, as well as fid-dles, banjos, and guitars. Concerts are presented Monday through Saturday at 7:30 P.M. in the center's 1,000-seat auditorium. Sunday-night gospel concerts are held once or twice a month through the season. Call (501) 269–3851 for a schedule.

The century-old Shannon Cabin at the center is open to visitors. It has a stone fireplace, homemade furniture, front and rear porches, and a sleeping loft typical of the rural log homes of the past century. Scheduled for demolition, it was brought to the center from Happy Hollow in Stone County. Tina Marie Wilcox, Ozark Folk Center herbalist, did the landscaping, planting an assortment of homestead flowers, herbs, and bushes around the cabin, the way a pioneer woman might have done.

Although the Ozark Folk Center Restaurant and Lodge is located in the middle of the state park, innkeeper June Burroughs takes care of you as though you were her personal guest. The octagonal cabins are built from native cedar and scattered around the grounds. Three sliding glass doors let in the breeze and a wide view of the trees outside, and the dining room serves traditional southern cooking—beans and ham, greens, and cornbread. Call (501) 269–3871 for room reservations.

An underground stream flows into Blanchard Springs Caverns, which is just 14 miles north of Mountain View off Highway 5/9/14 at the town of Sylamore (where Highway 5/9/14 splits), then east on Highway 14. The water emerges as Sylamore Creek, winding its way through the Ozark National Forest to the White River. It is an important part of the cavern; 216 feet beneath the lush green of the Ozark National Forest lies the underground world of massive stalactites and towering sandstone columns, sculpted by water and time and home to blind salamanders and albino crayfish. This is a living cave because the continuous water supply keeps the formations growing. The uppermost caverns consist of two huge rooms, the Cathedral Room and the Coral Room, which are large enough to hold several football fields each. The explored part of the lower section, where the river flows, is almost 5 miles long.

The Dripstone Trail passes though the uppermost part of the caverns for 0.7 mile with stone curbs or handrails. Every type of calcite formation can be found in the limestone caves—stalactites, stalagmites, hollow soda straws, massive flowstones, and giant columns in colors ranging from snow white to dark brown because of the varied minerals found in the deposits.

The Discovery Trail—discovered when someone fell through a hole in the floor—is 1.2 mile long and has more than 600 steps that take you deeper into the caverns, where there are water-carved passages, a cave stream, and the natural entrance. One spot looks as though billions of diamonds had spilled into the cavern, the crystals sparkling in the lights. Granted, it's a well-known tourist spot, but it would be a shame to miss it. It is one of the most beautiful caves in the world. For information call the U.S. Forest Service at (501) 757–2211.

Traveling west on Highway 66 from Mountain View leads to Timbo, the hometown of Jimmy Driftwood. Here **Ozark Mountain Trail Rides** invites you to take your horse on vacation in the Ozark Mountains. Talk about getting off the beaten path—Bob Roper has the way to do it: a week-long camp-out with guides to take you through some Ozark wilderness that can't be seen by car. Most of the trail is old logging roads crossing Roasting Ear Creek and other streams. Bring your favorite steed to the permanent camp on Roasting Ear Creek between Mountain View and Leslie where each day begins and ends at the campsite, which has electricity and a bathhouse; all you need is your horse and sleeping gear. Meals are served in a screened dining room, and you can buy hay and sweet feed for your mount. The end of the trail for riders is not the end of the fun, though. The campsite has a dance floor and live music. Dancing until midnight is part of the fun, and on Thursday night an auctioneer begins his chant to sell anything you have to sell. The rides are in April, June, and October, and advance reservations are necessary; call (501) 746–4300. The week-long trail rides cost $130 for adults, with prices ranging down from $100 for children under twelve, $75 for children under six, and $25 for children under three. To find the place, turn off of Highway 66 to Highway 263 North at Timbo.

On top of Fox Mountain is the small, small town of Fox (two grocery stores and a post office) on Highway 263. Getting to Fox is about an hour's drive from Mountain View, with two ways to get there. One is to travel on scenic Highway 66 to Highway 263, but this route has a terror of a hairpin turn onto Highway 263 that you might find exciting if you are an Ozark Mountain Daredevil driver. Or try Highway 9 south to Highway 263. This is a more pastoral drive along a road of soft hills lined with old barns. There are about five artists living in the area; some work at the Ozark Folk Center, others don't, and they are a challenge to find.

Fox Mountain Pottery is the home shop of Joe and Terri Bruhin, the weaver you met at the Ozark Folk Center. Joe is a potter whose pride and joy is a Noborigama-type, three-chambered, climbing natural-draft-wood-fired kiln ("I don't think there's another one like it in the state" remarks Terri). Here he creates one-of-a-kind stoneware and porcelain pottery, everything from traditional casseroles and mugs to large urns that stand 2 feet tall. The kiln reaches temperatures of 2,500 degrees, so the resulting high-fired pottery is good in the oven, microwave, or kitchens on Mercury or Venus. It's pottery meant to be used, as well as being original artwork. To find the shop once you're in Fox, turn onto the dirt road next to the post office and begin the trek into the hills. Call Joe for directions at (501) 363–4264.

Joe can also direct you to the other craftspeople around Fox—a silversmith, a needlepoint artist, a woodworker who makes fishing lures, and a couple who do woodworking and weaving. Terri Bruhin can usually be found at the Ozark Folk Center in the weavers' shop, where she weaves contemporary and traditional lace-weave table linens, bread basket liners, and such. She also makes rag rugs and contemporary clothing.

Four miles west of Fox on unpaved County Road 2 lies **Meadowcreek Environmental Center,** at 1 Meadowcreek Road, a 1,500-acre, nonprofit environmental education center offering programs for all ages in alternative energy, ecology, and agriculture. Meadowcreek consists of an old farm, a cluster of new buildings, and a small staff. But the show-and-tell philosophy of "using the earth without using it up" makes the place a combination think tank, science camp, and workshop. Interns from colleges as far away as the Soviet Academy of Sciences in Puschino study here. Last year students from more than a hundred colleges—including Princeton, Vassar, and the London School of Economics—came to Meadowcreek to see the solar design of the oak and stone conference center, with its motion-sensor light switches automatically turning off the lights when the room is empty.

Meadowcreek has a cattle operation as well as a terrace project with a one-and-one-half acre contoured slope that is operated as a "closed system," with nutrient cycling, ecological pest control, and planned cropping. The conference center kitchen utilizes the produce from the terraces. Waste is recycled to the soil through composting. It is a place that can awaken in each person a sense of global responsibility and help develop models that can be used in communities around the world. It is also home to the state's largest solar photovoltaic power system, whose blue solar panels draw in energy from the sun and generate electricity to the 300-acre farm without air pollution. A profitable crop of shiitake mushrooms in a growing medium of low-grade sweet-gum logs helps support the center. Call ahead to arrange for a tour: (501) 363–4500.

Calico Rock is a pretty little town of about 1,000 people, located on the bluffs of the White River north of Mountain View on Highway 5. The many colors of the sheer vertical cliffs along the river make it easy to see how the town got its name—steamship captains used to say, "Stop by them calico rocks," because it was the northernmost accessible port for steamboats in the spring of the year—and the name stuck. There's a view of the river from Main Street, and the old buildings, made of the colored rock and brick, reflect the 1920s and 1930s, when the railroad and sawmills that had made the town led to its destruction: A passing locomotive sparked a fire on a warehouse roof, and Main Street was destroyed. The town was rebuilt, however, and now the buildings are filled with crafts, collectibles, and antiques shops.

The mills can still be seen in the older part of town, and wood homes of the 1920s and 1930s perch on the river bluffs. Darlene Nelson and her daughter Paula Langston have restored the 1923 **River View Hotel** 1 block from the Main Street of Calico Rock. The white cement block hotel (not fancy but built for railroad workers who passed through the town in the 1920s when the woodmills were active) is now a B & B. It is filled with antiques and collectibles of the 1920s, has iron beds in some rooms and oak mission furniture in others, and overlooks the White River. Private baths are found in each room, some with tubs and some with showers. Each room is different; the prices range from $30 to $48 and include breakfasts of biscuits, sausage, fruit, sweet rolls, or whatever else strikes the cook's fancy. Breakfast is served buffet-style in the small sunroom off the lobby. You can make reservations by calling (501) 297–8208 or the Arkansas and Ozarks Bed and Breakfast Reservation Service.

Carolyn and Christian Eck operate the Arkansas and Ozarks Bed and Breakfast Reservation Service. Carolyn is quite knowledgeable about the area and a good person to see first. Using this service is the fastest way to book rooms for a trip and much easier on your phone bill than calling every B & B along the route. Several B & Bs are in the Calico Rock area and are owned by Carolyn and her husband. You can usually find her at the shops they own—The

Landing and Calico Country—both across the street from the River View Hotel. Call (501) 297–8211 (days) or 297–8764.

Probably the most romantic idea for a bed and breakfast is the Eck's two log cabins surrounded by the Ozark National Forest. These are a mile and a half from anywhere. In fact, after you reach the property, it is still a half-mile of woods to the cabins. Talk about a perfect location for a honeymoon hideaway! There are hiking trails and mountains to climb. Each cabin has a sleeping loft and a wood-burning stove, and both are unhosted for maximum privacy but provided with coffee and homemade fruit bread (the pumpkin bread is a favorite)—all for $42.50, plus $10.00 for each additional person.

If that's a little too much privacy for your taste, then the Eck's Forest Home Lodge, perched on a bluff overlooking the clear White River, might be more your style. Guests enjoy not only satellite television but a large, three-keyboard organ in the contemporary home, which is decorated with stained glass. A country breakfast includes homemade breads and a hearty main dish and is served on a deck outside your room. Rates are $35; call Arkansas and Ozarks Bed and Breakfast Reservation Service at (501) 297–8764.

Northwest of Calico Rock on Highway 5 is the town of Norfork. The confluence of the North Fork and White rivers served as a changeover point for pioneers who followed the White River and then switched from boats to ox carts. The town of Norfork grew from that point.

The **Wolf House,** built somewhere between 1809 and 1825, is off Highway 5 in Norfork. It was the home of Major Jacob Wolf, sent as an Indian agent by President Thomas Jefferson. For more than a half-century it served as a courthouse, post office, and stage and steamboat stop. The historic house, said to be the oldest remaining log cabin in the state, is open for tours during the warm months and contains antiques and memorabilia dating from the 1700s—more than 400 pieces of interesting relics and furniture of the time, including items as unusual as a rare 1870 hanging mousetrap, a glass parlor flytrap, and an 1860 ruffle iron for ironing ruffles on ladies' dresses. Built by black and Native American craftsmen, the handmade bricks of clay—dug and fired on the property—compose the four fireplaces and two chimneys. Half-dovetailed notched logs and original wrought iron hinges, as well as the lock-raftered roof (no ridgepole is used), give fascinat-

The Wolf House

ing insight into the labor and time required for the home to expand—the family grew to include the six children of two wives. Volunteers have the house open from 9:00 A.M. to 5:00 P.M. Monday through Saturday from April 15 to October 15. There is a craft shop next door designed to match the house. To find the house, take Highway 5 South 0.25 mile past the North Fork River Bridge.

Follow Highway 5 north toward Mountain Home but turn at County Road 68 to find a mountain retreat with a country club setting. **P.J.'s Lodge** sits on the banks of the White River overlooking the Ozarks National Forest. Owners Paul and Joyce Campbell designed and built the ten-room lodge, which attracts fishermen and vacationers from many other states. Each guest room opens into a courtyard, and each has a double bed and a twin bed, as well as a private bath and shower. The lodge is done in a 1930s style, its large lounge and dining room surrounded with windows overlooking the river and a manicured lawn.

The lodge's lounge is a place to "kick back and relax," according to Joyce. In no time people have their feet up on the couch and feel right at home. The hardwood floors and overstuffed furniture give the lounge a kind of western feel. It has a "BYOB" bar with mix—where people can fix their own drinks—and a television set. There's even a nightly fly-tying demonstration for fishermen. The center of attention in the lounge is Dancer, a blue and gold hook-bill parrot, a macaw, who is only ten years old—that's about the same as a human ten-year-old, because parrots live to be about eighty years old. Joyce says that if Dancer isn't the center of attention, he soon makes himself noticed.

Family-style, home-cooked meals with fresh-baked breads and European desserts like strudels and mocha or raspberry cakes—some fourteen different kinds of desserts, all made from scratch, are served in the large, antiques-furnished dining room. A complete breakfast is part of the plan—the cost is $65.00, plus $25.00 for each additional person—and dinner is $13.95. Call Arkansas and Ozarks Bed and Breakfast Reservation Service at (501) 297–8764, or call the lodge at (501) 499–7500 and Joyce can help you arrange float trips or trips to scout out antiques and crafts in the area. County Road 68 dead-ends into the quiet river, and the lodge is right there. You can't miss it.

But instead of going north, you can leave Highway 5, turning onto Highway 126 at Norfork and following it west to Gassville on Highway 62. Here Paul Johnson and his wife, Reita, have completely restored a hundred-year-old health lodge and turned it into a fine bed-and-breakfast. The Lithia Springs Bed and Breakfast Lodge was featured on the "Good Morning America" television show while the lodge was being restored. The two-story frame lodge was stripped to its shell and got all-new walls, plumbing, wiring, heating, and air-conditioning. It sits on thirty-nine acres of meadow and woods and reflects the original character of the health lodge, which was built so that people could relax and "take the waters" of the bicarbonate of lithium spring nearby, water that was bottled and sent all over the country.

Reita prepares a great breakfast specialty—a luscious Stuffed

French Bread (stuffed with cream cheese and nuts) covered with an orange sauce. If that is too rich for you, she always has health-ful—and scrumptious—homemade bran and raisin muffins on hand. Five rooms are available upstairs, three with private baths and showers and two with shared baths that have old-fashioned tubs and sinks. The lodge has a craft shop, too, featuring the woodwork and clocks Paul makes, as well as the many crafts Reita fashions. She dresses bears, makes potpourri, and excels at several kinds of stitchery. Reservations can be made through Arkansas and Ozarks Bed and Breakfast Service at (501) 297–8764 or by calling the lodge at (501) 435–6100. Room prices are from $37 to $40.

If trout dimpling around you in a cold stream is your idea of heaven, then Ken and Judy Epperson at the Cotter-Trout Dock in Cotter, the town just west of Gassville on Highway 345, can arrange float trips on the Buffalo, North Fork, or White rivers. Both single-day floats, covering 15 to 20 miles of river, and overnight camp trips are available. All trips carry a guide and food. The overnight trips have a commissary boat operated by the cook and range from two to six days. You need bring only your fishing tackle and personal effects; everything else is supplied, and floats are tailored to your individual requirements. Guides with many years on the river ("We've been here as long as the trout have," says Judy) know where to fish. The cost is about $75 per person per day for day trips. Overnight trips on the White River are about $132.50 each, with a minimum of four people and two days. The same kind of trip on the Buffalo River, where the smallmouth live, is $152.50, but fishing is good only April through June. Call (501) 435–6525 to arrange trips.

The dock is under the historical Rainbow Arch Bridge on High-way 62B at Cotter. Built in 1930 at a cost of $500,000, the cement bridge, with its five rainbow stands, is very rare. It was the first bridge across the White River and is listed on the National Register of Historic Places.

If you are following Highway 62 west toward Harrison, you will find a couple of good B & Bs. The Red Raven Inn, near the Buffalo River at Highways 62 and 14 South near Yellville, is the perfect base for float trips. Don and Cam Semelsberger are hosts at the inn, which sits right on the banks of Crooked Creek (the creek is full of smallmouth bass). The stately Queen Anne–style, turn-of-the-century inn, with its wraparound porch, has seven bedrooms, all with private baths and each decorated in a different theme. The prices range from $43 to $63 and include breakfast—Don's *aebel-skivers* (a Danish pancake with red raspberry jam) or Belgian waffles. You can invite local guests to join you for breakfast for $5.00. There is even a honeymoon suite for $63. Call (501) 449–5168.

The Corn Cob Inn was built as a general store for the mining community of Everton, off Highway 62 near Harrison. Then it became a corncob pipe factory. Now it is Leon McLean's comfortable native-stone home on eighteen acres. There are three bedrooms upstairs and two downstairs; three have shared baths. The price of $25 to $35 includes breakfast, and dinner can also be arranged. Leon's mother, Louise, is the cook, and she turns out a "good ole country breakfast" of biscuits with sausage, gravy, eggs, and the works. The view from the porch and second-story bedrooms is of beautiful Clear Creek, which runs by the front door. Plenty of hiking trails are nearby, and the creek has a private swimming beach. Call (501) 429–6545.

Highway 62 rolls into Harrison, the center of a scenic resort community in the valley of Crooked Creek. If this is the end of the day for you, find the Hathaway House "Fernsides" Bed and Breakfast at 322 West Ridge. This 1910 Craftsman–style cottage lets you experience a bit of English charm with period antiques. Owner Jan Younes has five large guest rooms with private and semiprivate baths. The home is only a block from downtown, on a hill overlooking the area.

The place was named Fernsides by the original owners, as was the custom of the day, but Jan didn't discover that interesting bit of history until she had already named the 2-story cobblestone and English-timber home Hathaway House. Breakfast is usually an egg casserole or quiche with fresh fruit and muffins. Rooms go for $75 with a private bath or $65 with a semiprivate bath; the prices go down to $65 and $55, respectively, in November. Call (501) 741–3321 or 741–9546 for reservations.

Mountain Pines Cabin, a romantic mountaintop hideaway in Hill Top, 12 miles southwest of Harrison on Highway 43 South, is a lovingly restored, hand-hewn, 2-story log cabin with three bedrooms, two baths, a kitchen, a rock fireplace, and several spectacular views from the deck—or through the 15-foot-high glass wall across the south side of the cabin—of 116 acres of forest. Karin and Mike Nabors found the beauty—built as a barn in the 1850s—and moved it to Gaither Mountain. Then they restored it, log by massive log, on a spot overlooking Cecil Cove and the Buffalo National River and surrounded by hundreds of acres of hardwood forest and pines. The cabin is completely hidden in the wilderness and filled with primitive antiques and quilts. There's even a handmade rocker on the front porch. The old puncheon floors (made from logs that were split in half) are curved on the underneath side, smooth on top, and composed of trees split and carried to the site. Nothing is really level, and the colors in the hardwood floor vary with the kind of tree used.

The kitchen is more modern, if you can call it that. Home to a 1932 electric stove and refrigerator, the kitchen also has a modern coffeepot to go with the great breakfast Karin delivers in the morning—puff pancakes or Dutch babies (sort of like German pancakes) with fresh applesauce, bananas and honey, strawberries, or whatever other berries happen to be in season. When the season is right, there are fresh huckleberries, black raspberries, or blackberries all over the place that you can pick yourself. Guests are greeted with a sweet baked treat of some type. The weathered-gray cabin is brightened by dried flowers hanging in the windows; a catwalk over the entrance joins the two bedrooms on the second floor. The cabin is rented to one family at a time. It's small enough (and certainly private enough) for a honeymoon, yet ample enough for a small family get-together as well.

There are miles of trails going to spots like Inspiration Point. This trail leads along a high bluff with a view of the valley; another takes you to a 60-foot summer waterfall. The deck on the back of the cabin is high in the air, looking into the valley of tall pine trees and rock bluffs; there's nothing but wilderness for 20 miles, with the river and mountains in the distance. The cabin is $89 per night plus $10 for extra people over twelve years old. Call (501) 420–3575 for reservations and instructions on how to get there.

It seems as though the mountains pop up as suddenly as spring mushrooms around here once you cross the border from Missouri—everywhere a view on Highway 65. There can be no doubt that this is Arkansas.

Aunt Shirley's Sleeping Loft Bed and Breakfast is near Omaha on Highway 65—and yes, there is a real sleeping loft, one that will sleep five people. But even better, the loft is in a cabin next to the main house, so guests have complete privacy. The cabin can handle an entire family with three double beds, a daybed, and a quaint country bedroom on the main floor; the cabin also has such modern conveniences as a small refrigerator, a microwave, and a color television set to accompany the country motif. A complimentary bottle of champagne greets honeymooners. Shirley and Buddy LeBleu own the eighty lovely mountaintop acres. A couple of swings hang from the trees out front, and rockers on the porch catch the cool mountain breezes. There are quiet walkways, bikes for borrowing, and views everywhere. With plenty of space for the kids to run free, Aunt Shirley's is far away from anywhere and anything. And though far from the madding crowd, the B & B is near enough to Branson, Missouri, and its fabulous collection of country music theaters to make it a good place to stay if Branson is too hectic and crowded (which it is).

Children are welcome at this open, country hideout. In fact when children are along, "Aunt" Shirley fixes a favorite from her Arkansas childhood, chocolate milk gravy, to go on the homemade country biscuits she serves for breakfast. A big country breakfast with fresh biscuits and gravy, grits, and eggs is an everyday thing, but if you stay a week, Shirley fixes her specialty—Dutch pancakes (these look like cream puffs when they come out of the oven and are filled with blueberries and topped with whipped cream).

The loft is available by chance or reservation but only to one family at a time. There's a room in the main house (with a waterbed) for extra people. Find Boone County Road 15 east off Highway 65—it winds about 3.5 miles through the woods—or call (501) 426–5408.

To get to the Bull Shoals Lake area, take Highway 14 from Omaha back toward Yellville; then take Highway 178 north to the lake area. Fishing on the lakes and rivers below the Bull Shoals Dam near Mountain Home makes this region popular with fishing enthusiasts. The White and North Fork rivers provide perfect trout waters for 100 miles downstream. The silver flash glimmering in the summer sunlight is often a record-threatening catch, and all the state trout records and a new world record (a thirty-eight-pound, nine-ounce German brown trout caught in 1988) reside here.

Just east of the town of Bull Shoals are Lakeview and the **Concert Vineyards Winery,** at 1 Old Ferry Road, owned by Dr. Larry and Lou Annis Kelley. Their daughter Laura is a winemaker. The winery is on eighteen acres containing some 200 varieties of grapes, predominately the Cynthiana, a native Arkansas grape. All the wines are blends, and they come in several styles, some of which won bronze medals in the Eastern International Wine Competition in New York. The winery has been open since June 1990, but Dr. Kelley has been growing grapes in the vineyards since 1975, starting from the ground up, so to speak, to blend these wines. The tasting room is open from 10:00 A.M. to 6:00 P.M. Monday through Saturday and from 1:00 to 5:00 P.M. on Sunday. Tours of the winery can be made by appointment; call (501) 431–9463.

Due east of Lakeview on Highway 178 is the town of Mountain Home. Mountain Home Country Inn, at 1501 Highway 201 North, is a turn-of-the-century, 1905 Colonial-style house furnished with antiques and wicker. It has a large deck and a "sitting porch" across the front, where hosts Ellen and Bob Ritlinger greet guests with complimentary wine or soft drinks. The house is surrounded by huge black oak trees and sits on an acre of ground. The view from the shaded back deck is of Arkansas farmland. The inn is only a mile from town, and guests have use of the high-ceilinged living room—with its open fireplace—for visiting. Four rooms are available, some with private baths, and prices range from $35 to $40. Breakfast, featuring Belgian waffles, real Wisconsin maple syrup, and blueberries with whipped cream or homemade muffins and baked eggs, is served in the glass-enclosed breakfast room. You can make reservations through Arkansas and Ozarks Bed and Breakfast Service at (501) 297–8764.

If you travel down Highway 62, you'll find about fifteen antiques, collectibles, and crafts shops, as well as several good eating places. Start shopping at **Country Reflections,** owned by Cindy and Ken Duntman and located at 1015 Highway 62 Southwest. Cindy has turned an old house into a storefront shop and has four rooms of unusual things: old record albums in good shape, antiques, handmade baby clothes (including a cute seersucker suit for baby boys), wire gift items (rolling pin holders, rug beaters), pottery, used furniture—almost anything you can think of. Cindy has lived here since 1973; she and Ken are in the shop from 9:00 A.M. to 5:00 P.M. Monday through Friday and from 9:00 A.M. to 4:00 P.M. Saturday and enjoy directing people to interesting places in the area. Call (501) 425–7177.

Nearby is Pat Graves's **Country Cottage Tea Room,** a Victorian tearoom at 1634 Highway 62 Southwest. The single-story building is blue with white gingerbread trim, and the interior is done English-style, with European lace window curtains, rose-colored chairs, teal linens, and fresh flowers on each table. The three dining rooms are in soft colors with hand-stenciled trim. The raspberry tea and tiny cranberry muffins with citrus butter accompany a number of crepes (seafood, enchilada beef, asparagus) and quiches. The creamy carrot soup is a must-try item and a favorite. Fruit with poppy seed dressing or salad comes with each meal. In fact there are six different salads and sandwiches. And the desserts—oh my, the desserts: Black Forest parfait; apple cobbler crepe with fresh Jonathan apples, currants, walnuts, caramel sauce, and whipped cream; or turtle cheesecake. The gift shop sells European lace by the yard. Hours are from 11:00 A.M. to 3:00 P.M. Monday through Friday; call (501) 425–2946 for more information.

Now Bobbie Sue's Dawg House is a very different kind of place, certainly not a tearoom. Located in a strip shopping center on Highway 62 East, this eatery is a well-kept secret—a lot of locals haven't even discovered it—and the kind of place you might pass by without noticing. But people who do know about it head there on Wednesday at noon for the barbecued ribs. Usually boneless, these are cut from the end of the loin and are spicy and succulent. There is homemade bread for soaking up the sauce, as well as homemade beans and potato salad. Owners Bobbie McMillan and Sue Kasinger peel potatoes and make everything from scratch. There's a daily lunch special, and breakfast draws a crowd, too. Sue says, "We give everyone a hard time so they'll feel at home." It has a full bar, so if you want to "be in the Dawg House," it's open Monday through Friday, 6:30 A.M. to 8:00 P.M., at 313 Forest (1300 Highway 62 East); call (501) 425–2923.

Spring River Area

If you've headed northeast from Mountain Home, take Highways 62 and 9 to Mammoth Springs, so named because of its size, not because of any prehistoric elephant remains. It is the outlet of a subterranean river, and legend has it that the spring was found when an Indian chief dug a grave for his son, who had died searching for water during a drought. The Spring River is created by the flow from Mammoth Spring in the foothills; it is one of the largest natural waterflows in the nation and, because of a constant release from the huge natural spring—nine million gallons each hour—has canoeing and trout fishing year-round.

The **Roseland Inn** in the Morris-Pace House in Mammoth Springs is on six lots of tree-shaded yard, surrounded by the original wrought iron fence. There are leaded glass windows, a carved oak mantel, and pocket doors decorating this 1906 Colonial Revival home at 570 Bethel Street. The owner and hostess is Jean Pace, formerly mayor and now president of the Chamber of Commerce of this sleepy little Ozark town that is home to about 1,100 people. Jean lives in the house next door but fixes breakfast, late-afternoon dessert, and tea as part of the hospitality in the carefully restored, four-bedroom house. The first floor has a dining room, a double parlor, and a spring room where the original cistern still pumps water. The kitchen has what was surely, in 1908, a state-of-the-art zinc metal sink and original cabinets. A gazebo in the yard and a large porch across the front of the house have rockers for late-evening sitting. Rooms are $30 to $35; call (501) 625-3378 for reservations.

There's plenty to do in Mammoth Springs during the spring, summer, and fall months. For example, every Thursday night square dancing takes place downtown, and every Friday night a free musical show with a live band made up of local people plays good country music. In fact it's an open-mike arrangement, so if you want to get up there and show off your own banjo or fiddlin' skills, the crowd welcomes you. On Saturday night is the two-step dance, also with a live band.

The town is country music crazy because of George D. Hay, the founder of the Grand Ole Opry. He traveled to the springs in the 1920s as a reporter with the *Commercial Appeal* in Memphis. Invited to a hoedown, Hay was inspired by the local band that played well into the night and by the crowd that stayed up with it. "No one in the world has ever had more fun than those Ozark mountaineers did that night," Hay said. "It stuck with me until the idea became the Grand Ole Opry. . . . It's as fundamental as sunshine and rain, snow and wind and the light of the moon peeping through the trees. . . . [I]t'll be there long after you and I have passed out of this picture." And so it is. Every Labor Day weekend the town now has the "Solemn Old Judge Days" celebration to remember that enthusiasm—it's a regular hoedown with jig dancing and all. Then Saturday night the townfolk get very serious about the flattop guitar and fiddle contest that anyone can enter; the winner is guaranteed a spot at Fanfare in Nashville—the Grand Masters' fiddle contest.

Mammoth Springs is known for its antiques shopping, and bargains are plentiful. Michael's Antiques is just one example. It consists of two stores, with two floors each of antiques and used furniture, situated on Main Street downtown. Call (501) 625-3254.

The Spring River flows from Mammoth Springs to Hardy. On the banks of the Spring River, the historic village of Hardy is where professional artists have settled and trout fishermen and canoes have filled the summertime river for more than a century. The main street is filled with turn-of-the-century storefronts that have been converted into a collection of antiques, crafts, and gift shops. Though the restored area is not big enough to tire you, it does hold more than fifty or sixty shops full of antiques, collectibles, and most unusual things in the 3 blocks of Main Street known as "Old Hardy Town." Most of the buildings have no street numbers on them, but these are in order from School Street north to Kelley Street.

The **Old Stone House Bed and Breakfast** is right on Main and School streets and within easy walking distance to all shops. It is owned by Peggy and David Johnson. The 2-story, native-stone house has two large porches along the front and one side. A jumbo country rocker on the front porch overlooks a hedge of simplicity roses, and the side porch has white wicker furniture. Located at 511 Main Street, the establishment is just across the street from the Spring River, where there are always rafts, canoes, or kayaks floating by. Two bedrooms and baths are on the second floor, where vaulted ceilings and ceiling fans move cool air; antiques grace both these and the three bedrooms and baths on the first floor. Guests can use the living room, and the Johnsons have an extensive library of books, CDs, tapes, and board games. Coffee trays are brought to the rooms or to the side porch for early risers, and brunch is served about 9:00 A.M.—homemade granola and fresh fruit with homemade bread or muffins and fresh strawberry butter for the diet conscious and something really decadent like baked German apple pancakes for the rest of us. ("You don't have to eat it all," says Peggy.) Rooms are $45 during the week, and $55 on weekends. Call (501) 856-2983 for reservations.

Local folklorist Wayne Lowder and his wife, Karen, display two floors of handmade crafts by area artisans at the Ozark Classic

Crafts Mall at 617 Main Street. Wayne makes wood-carved flutes, known as Indian Serenade flutes, and plays them. Each flute takes about thirty hours' work to reach the right tone. Weekly demonstrations of such crafts as woodworking, silversmithing, rug weaving, tatting, and blacksmithing go on during the season. Wayne also does magic tricks for children, and he lives up to the title folklorist by telling amusing tales to anyone who wanders in. The mall is open seven days a week, from 9:00 A.M. to 5:00 P.M. Monday through Saturday and from 11:00 A.M. to 4:00 P.M. Sunday. Call (501) 856–2892.

Jeff and Debbie Kamps' **Flat Creek Dulcimer Shop** is at 644 Main Street. Jeff's mountain dulcimers are entirely handcrafted in the shop, along with door harps and other crafts. But the dulcimers and dulcimer tapes are what bring folks in. The instruments are made of walnut and butternut and cost $219, a price that includes a case, an instruction book, and two lessons; if you live somewhere else, the Kamps will substitute free shipping for the two lessons. Jeff's whole family plays the dulcimer. His son Aaron and daughter Sarah both work in the glass-front workshop, and you can watch them. Call (501) 856–2992 for more information.

Dale and Liane Maddox create **Hardy Pottery** at 701 Main Street and sell it along with hand-forged fireplace sets, white oak baskets, porch swings, wooden toys, hand-tied brooms, and a host of other crafts items. The pottery is both functional—mugs, serving pieces, canisters—and decorative—lamps, vases. Dale works at the potter's wheel at the back of the shop, and visitors are invited to watch him there. Liane has a workshop at their home where she develops new designs. The shop is open from 9:00 A.M. to 5:00 P.M. Monday through Saturday; call (501) 856–3735.

David Pickens's **Naturals,** at 724 Main Street, is a unique enterprise offering exotic butterflies, shells, and scrimshaw in a storefront shop in what is actually the old Sharp County Courthouse building. David's office is in the old vault, complete with steel door and bars on the windows. The jail is still out back. David does wood-carvings, caricatures, birds, and weathervanes, and his shop features artists from around the state. There's an art gallery with no end of interesting things to see, such as butterflies brought in from all over the world and mounted in shadowboxes and frames, as well as shells as big as the 30-inch triton trumpet.

The shop is open from 9:00 A.M. to 5:00 P.M. seven days a week, year-round. Call (501) 856–2898 for more information.

East of Hardy on Highway 175 is the town of Cherokee Village, home of the **Arkansas Indian Culture Center and Folklore Museum** in the center of this modern recreational community. All 536 streets, seven lakes, and public facilities of the community are named in honor of Native American tribes and leaders. (The community has two really fine golf courses, too.) The museum traces the history, culture, and food of the Americans native to Arkansas from prehistoric times of the Paleolithic period (10,000 B.C.) to the 1830s, as well as tribes passing through the state on the Trail of Tears. Hands-on exhibits allow you to try grinding corn the Indian way. Knowledgeable Native American staff members will show you tribal artifacts, including those of the Quapaw, Osage, Caddo, Cherokee, Shawnee, and Delaware. The museum, situated in the Cherokee Town Center, is open daily from 9:00 A.M. (11:00 A.M. Sundays) to 5:00 P.M. (November–March, opens at 10:00 A.M.). Admission to this museum, which is located along a branch of the Trail of Tears, is free. There's a gift shop to browse through, with items ranging from beaded earrings to blankets. Call (501) 257–2442 for more information.

The town of Maynard lies by the Missouri border, north and east of Hardy and Cherokee Village. If you happen to pass through Maynard in September, you will become part of the Pioneer Days Festival, with its hour-long parade, dress revues, frontier games, and free musicals. This little town—population 381—swells to beyond 6,000 for the two-day event, which includes a craft festival, a chicken and dumpling dinner, a gospel sing, and a bluegrass music festival in the park.

The **Maynard Pioneer Museum** is housed in a century-old log cabin not far from the business district of this small town. The museum is on Highway 328 and Spring Street, and a city park surrounds it. The inside depicts a typical rural home of the late 1800s, with handmade furnishings, old photos, tools, and heirloom needlework; a muzzle-loader rifle hangs over the fireplace. The museum, said to be one of the finest pioneer museums in the region, is open May through September from 10:00 A.M. to 4:00 P.M. Tuesday through Saturday and from 1:00 to 4:00 P.M. Sunday, though you can see the museum just about anytime by calling Bea Hearn at City Hall (501–647–2701) or the park chairman, Lee Hearn, at (501) 647–2285. No admission is charged.

South of Maynard, Susan Reed and her husband grow wheat on their 400-acre farm outside of Walnut Ridge, south of Pocahontas on Highway 67. But at **Reed's Wheatweavings** Susan does more than just grow wheat: She weaves the stalks into beautiful designs. Her weavings, ranging from the usual sheaves (also called shocks) to wall hangings, house blessings, and useful items like napkin rings—some sixty different designs—are all originals. To see Susan's work, drive north 7 miles on Highway 67 to a bright blue building, turn right onto the gravel road, and go 1 mile to the first house. Call Susan first at (501) 892–3157.

Crowley's Ridge and the Delta

One of the surprises of this part of the Mississippi Delta is that it has hills. Rising abruptly above the Delta region is a narrow band of gently rolling hills known as Crowley's Ridge; stretching north to south, it breaks the flat plains and is one of the great oddities of the world. It extends nearly 210 miles from the northeast corner of the state to the Mississippi River at Helena and covers a half-million acres. This tree-blanketed hill was formed by wind and water over millions of years just prior to the Ice Age, when the Mississippi and Ohio rivers cut vast trenches into the great plains of eastern Arkansas. The ridge was an island left when the two rivers retreated to the west.

The "highland" area of the ridge and the Ozark foothills, a region bounded by I–40 and Highway 167, contains a cluster of state parks, eleven of them to be exact, including two state museums and a memorial. Sixteen miles east of Crowley's Ridge State Park is downtown Paragould. But it's not called downtown anymore. The townsfolk decided that "uptown" sounded more, well, uptown than downtown, and so downtown Paragould is now called uptown Paragould. The pride of the town is a lighted mural of an old steam engine and depot. When driving on the Highway 412 overpass, you can look down into uptown Paragould.

In uptown Paragould, in an old service station under that overpass, is Dan's Duck-In. The specialties at Dan's are the sandwiches, and a favorite everyone talks about is called the Duck-In Special—a sandwich on thin white bread with ham, turkey, and cheese that's dipped in batter and deep-fried, then sprinkled with powdered sugar and served with marmalade. That sounds weird, but it is really good with a cold beer. Really. The Duck-In, located at 318 Second Street, is open Monday through Saturday from 11:00 A.M. to 11:00 P.M.; call (501) 236–1874.

Competing with the Duck-In in the sandwich department is the Hamburger Station at 110 East Main Street, home of the famous "hum-burger" with grilled onion, a burger so good it was mentioned in *USA Today* as one of the best hamburgers in the country. Dorothy Biddick and Marky Collun are the owners. Since its beginning in 1985, Hamburger Station has served sandwiches that rate high on the charts in this fast-food world: a roast turkey sandwich on a sesame-seed bun with bacon, cheese, lettuce, and tomato—and made from *real* turkey, roasted right there at the station. The roast beef sandwich is also made of "real beef," roasted in the station's oven. "No pressed-meat, imitation stuff here," notes Dorothy. The station also makes great shakes and malts. Hours are from 10:00 A.M. to 8:30 P.M. Monday through Saturday; call (501) 239–9956.

Farther south along Crowley's Ridge on Highway 140 is the town of Lepanto. A town that didn't have a paved road until 1937, Lepanto now has a four-room living model of the Delta's heritage called **Museum Lepanto, USA** at the intersection of Berney and Main streets. When the town was first founded, the only way into Lepanto was by boat on the Little River. Later the train came through, although it still took "all day to get out and another day to get back," according to Sue Chambers, the museum's director. This unique city shares the history of the Delta—the agricultural days, the Civil War and Indian conflicts, the Victorian era—in a museum supported entirely by the annual Terrapin Derby, a turtle race held the first Saturday of October for the past sixty-two years. (Of course, a craft fair, square dancing, and a parade are held, too.)

The people are proud of their history and show it in the town and the all-volunteer museum. The blacksmith shop, roofed with hand-hewn shingles, contains a huge iron anvil and all the tools and items created there, with a printed guide to identify and explain each one. A Victorian parlor, a general store full of supplies, and a doctor's office and barber shop have been rebuilt there, too. Fossilized Delta mud, old tintype photos, an early printing press, and one of the first Maytag washing machines, made in 1902, offer a perspective on the changes that swept the Delta region over the years. A collection of artifacts show the life of the Woodland Indians, who were native to the area. The museum is right there on Main Street and is open on Saturday and Sunday from noon to 4:00 P.M., April 1 to November 1; call (501) 475–2384. As long as Sue is the director, however, she will open it anytime, year-round—just wander into the Victorian Rose Antiques shop next door (two buildings full of glassware, china, and furniture) and use the phone there to call her at (501) 475–2591. Another manifestation of this town's pride is the mural at the four-way stop at Highway 140/135 depicting the town's Medal of Honor winner.

The **Hampson Museum State Park,** one of the state parks along Crowley's Ridge, features a most unusual museum, given to the state by James K. Hampson, a medical doctor with a successful practice who turned his boyhood fascination with arrowheads into the research and study of the physical remains of the early inhabitants of his family plantation, Nodena. He and his family excavated, studied, and inventoried the mounds and subsurface remains of a complex civilization that lived on the meander bend of the Mississippi River in a fifteen-acre palisaded village from A.D. 1350 to 1700. The result is an educational facility devoted to the study of these, the state's earliest inhabitants, and exhibits artifacts from the Late Mississippian period culture. The Nodena people were farmers who developed a civilization of art, religion, political structure, and trading networks. The park is 5 miles east of I–55 at the junction of Highway 61 and Lake Drive. Admission is $1.50 for adults and 75 cents for children six to twelve years old. Hours are from 9:00 A.M. to 5:00 P.M. Tuesday through Saturday. Call (501) 655–8622 for more information.

Traveling south along the Mississippi from the Nodena site will take you through the Wapanocca National Wildlife Refuge, 5,500 acres 5 miles west of the Mississippi River. The heart of the refuge is the 600-acre Wapanocca Lake, a shallow old oxbow of the once-meandering Mississippi River. Surrounded by 1,200 acres of cypress and willow swamp, the other two-thirds of the refuge is equally divided between remnants of once-extensive bottomland hardwood forest and cropland of the refuge's farm unit. A Nature Drive to observe a variety of birds and wildlife in each habitat is offered, and more than 228 species of birds are known to pass through here.

The town of West Memphis, south of the Wapanocca refuge, has all of the big-city excitement you could want. But if you wish to get away from the city and still be near enough to enjoy the greyhound races at the Southland Track, check out the twelve-acre **Snowden House Plantation Bed and Breakfast Resort** on Highway 147 at Horseshoe Lake near Hughes. Surrounded by boxwoods and magnolias and built in 1919, Snowden House is one of the largest and oldest plantation homes in the county. The lovely home has three bedrooms and three baths. The decor has the feel of an old plantation: Antiques grace each room; boxwoods line the drive. In fact the Snowdens and their maid are buried on the property.

It is more than a bed-and-breakfast now. The dining room is not just big—it's huge and seats fifty people. It is open for dinner on Friday and Saturday nights from 7:00 to 11:00 P.M., serving catfish and steak, grilled chicken, and grilled fish. Homemade bread and a wonderful dessert are included. The dining room and a glass-enclosed sunporch are on the main floor, but when the weather is right, a screened porch on the second floor, overlooking the lake, is an additional spot to enjoy dinner. Room prices range from $70 and include not only a big breakfast but swimming in the lake, paddleboating, nature trails, and fishing. Call (501) 339–3414 for reservations.

A bakery case piled high with homemade cookies, cinnamon rolls, and breads is the first thing you notice at **Clint's** on Highway 1 in Forrest City, northwest of Hughes on Highway 38. But owners Sue and Ron Willard also serve tasty meals, all with homemade breads. A breakfast specialty is Egg Glenda—ham, eggs, and biscuits topped with gravy. The place is famous for the gourmet eight-ounce burger with sautéed onion, mushrooms, and wafflecut fries. But the burger competes with all the other choices for sandwiches—and the selection will make you crazy if you hate to make decisions—with plenty of breads, together with toppings to adorn a variety of meats, cheeses, and vegetables. And speaking of vegetables, the veggie cheese pocket has fresh sprouts that are sprouting right there in the kitchen. (Sue had to check whether the current day's sprouts were big enough to use, yet.) The biscuits are so popular that Sue mails them to three other states where homesick people wait for them. Do not miss this place. Clint's is at 1132 North Washington. Call (501) 633–8811.

On Highway 1 north of Forrest City in Vanndale, **Granpa's Bargain Barn** has something for everyone who loves to hunt for treasure: antiques, farm tools, all kinds of glass—five million items at last count. And Harold Williams, "Granpa" to the tots in his family, says it's worth about $1 million dollars—the collection ranging from baseball cards to a Stradivarius violin (yes, a Stradivarius). But the violin is pretty common compared with the Honus Wagner baseball card, which is worth about $200,000. And everything is guaranteed, "even if they don't like the color of it," says Granpa. He's there seven days a week from 10:00 A.M. to 5:00 P.M. Call (501) 238-7441.

Highway 1 leads from Vanndale to Jonesboro, home to Nancy Blades Pottery, a combination studio-and-shop where Nancy makes both functional and decorative pieces in her several kilns. Nancy has been a potter for more than ten years and makes both wheel-thrown and handmade stoneware and porcelain pottery and jewelry. She will do custom orders for that special something you can't find anywhere else. She suggests you call ahead—(501) 931-9051—because her hours "vary wildly." The studio-and-shop is at 2705 North Culberhouse.

If feeding time has come upon you in Jonesboro, you are in luck. Sue's Kitchen, at 314 Main, is where Sue Williams seems to be able to please everyone with her "Country Collection." Although beef is the primary dinner specialty—tenderloins that range from delicate to huge—such entrees as red snapper and pasta brighten the menu, too. The chicken salad is unusual, to say the least—it contains whipped cream and grapes—but the desserts are the showstoppers. The Chocolate Fantasy is a mountain of chocolate: chocolate-chip cake with chocolate cream cheese frosting, ice cream, hot fudge sauce, whipped cream, toasted almond slivers, chocolate sprinkles, and a cherry. Sue's Kitchen is open for lunch from 11:00 A.M. to 1:30 P.M. Monday through Friday and for dinner from 5:30 to 8:30 P.M. every night except Sunday. Call (501) 972-5199.

Looking for something a little more continental? **Piero & Company Ristorante,** at 314 South Union, serves fine northern Italian food. And why not? Owner and chef Piero Trimarchi is from Florence. He and his wife, Sara, opened the restaurant in the basement of a 1905 building in downtown Jonesboro a few years ago. The Trimarchis are such perfectionists that they grow their own herbs and vegetables. In fact this year Piero's father visited from Florence and brought seeds for radicchio and arugala—salad greens very difficult to find around here—to plant in the Trimarchi garden. Such appetizers as grilled eggplant with tomato sauce and goat cheese, grilled leeks, or pepper salad begin the meals, which are planned around seasonal fresh vegetables. Delicate veal dishes with roasted potatoes and a most unusual white lasagna, with prosciutto and mushrooms await you.

Sara makes the desserts, and the most popular is one called "Sin." Of course, anything with a name that bad has to be good. It's a chocolate truffle cheesecake with chocolate topping, whipped cream with just a hint of Amaretto. If that's too rich for your taste, try the raspberry chocolate swirl or the lemon cheesecake that melts in your mouth. You are at Sara's mercy at dessert time; she fixes whatever strikes her fancy. Piero's is open for lunch and dinner but never on Sunday. Lunch is served from 11:00 A.M. to 2:00 P.M.; dinner, from 6:00 to 10:00 P.M. (but no lunch on Saturday). Call (501) 933–0034 to ask about the dessert du jour.

Off the Beaten Path in Northwest Arkansas

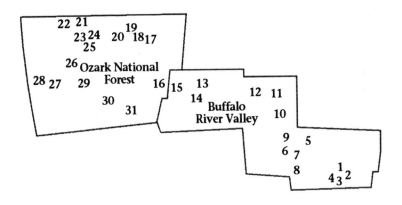

1. Heber Springs Outpost
2. Panache
3. Anderson House
4. The Captains' House
   Restaurant
5. B & G Bakery and Pizza
6. Pentacle Studio
7. Choctaw General Store
8. Traditions Coffee Shop and
   Arts and Crafts
9. Antiques Warehouse
10. Designs in Metal
11. Big Creek (MB) Ranch
12. Gilbert General Store
13. Brambly Hedge Cottage
    Bed and Breakfast
14. A Cabin in the Woods
15. The Champagne Flight
16. Images of Childhood
    puzzles

17. Saunders Memorial
    Museum
18. Currey Studio-Gallery
19. Eureka Springs
20. Harp's Grocery Store
21. Thorncrown Chapel
22. Wal-Mart Visitors Center
23. Antique and Art Gallery
24. Rogers
25. Boston Mountains Rail
    Excursion Company
26. War Eagle Mill
27. Mary Maestri's
28. Washington Street Bed and
    Breakfast
29. Johnson House Bed &
    Breakfast
30. Arkansas Air Museum
31. Holland Wild Flower Farm

Northwest Arkansas

The Buffalo River literally gets you off the beaten path and into a beautiful wilderness. It was the first National River Park established by Congress in 1972. Now about 12,000 canoes are rented during June and July, along with roughly the same number of private boats. Add the number of motorized fishermen and you have something like 50,000 folks floating down the 125-mile river. That's a lot of sunscreen. But the Buffalo cuts a path through some of the most unspoiled beauty in the country—towering limestone bluffs, white-water rapids, and natural wilderness—drawing campers, fishermen, and other folks bent on getting away from city stress.

Buffalo Point, at Highways 14 and 268, is the only fully developed park on the river. It offers camping, hiking trails, and rustic cabins and is run by the National Park Service. Outfitters can be found at every access point, in almost every town along the way.

The Buffalo River is a tributary of the majestic White River, where settlers built log cabins. These hardy settlers, isolated as they were from the rest of the world, developed a folk culture that still lives today in the backwoods and hollows along the creeks that feed the historic river.

It can reach 80 degrees or get plenty chilly by the middle of October, when dozens of arts and crafts fairs lure thousands of autumn tourists to the area. November and December have their own beauty; the winter has many mild days, with dramatic new scenes uncovered after foliage falls. Snow in these mountains can be from 2 inches to 2 feet, but it can also be gone quickly.

Buffalo River Valley

As you pass through the intersection of Highways 16 and 25 just outside of Heber Springs, you'll see the **Heber Springs Outpost.** It's just a convenience store—a huge mule and wagon on the roof makes it easy to spot, and a bright red antique bathtub full of iced soft drinks sits by the front door—but on Thursday there is freshly made seafood gumbo to go and on Friday the best crab chowder around. Of course, any other day of the week you can buy the gumbo or chowder by the pint, frozen, to take home. Wendel Baker is the chef, but manager Elizabeth Summerville keeps the outpost stocked with fresh seafood—lobster, shrimp, crab, or salmon—and Petit Jean meats for Heber residents. The store is open from 6:00 A.M. to 9:00 P.M. Monday through Thursday, until 9:30 P.M. on Friday and Saturday, and until 8:30 P.M. Sunday.

The Aromatique Factory, a multimillion-dollar business located on the outskirts of Heber Springs, started on a whim. Patti Upton created a pretty arrangement of pinecones and gumballs, brightened with green bay leaves, and gave it a Christmas scent with cinnamon, cloves, and such for her friend Sandra Horne's gift shop. The result, called "The Smell of Christmas," was a sellout hit. What started as a small business for the two women has grown to the Aromatique Factory, a corporation employing more than 400 persons on Highway 25 North in Heber Springs.

A showroom for the factory, called **Panache,** is filled with the lovely scents created here. Described as "A'romantic shop," it is part of the factory complex and carries the decorative room fragrances sold only in upscale gift shops and the finest department stores. It's a treat just to walk into the little shop and be bathed in the delicate scents. Choosing among them is fun, too. Now there are eleven scented mixtures of wood chips and botanicals, over a hundred ingredients in all, with scents romantically named "Smell of Spring"—a hyacinth-scented collection of bougainvillea; German statice in purple, pink, and white; bright green bay leaves; and curled poplar in mauve—or "Gentleman's Quarters" made up of "rugged, exotic botanicals" with a masculine, outdoorsman scent. All combine colors and textures artfully and carry a delicate but definite scent. Prices range from $7.50 for a small cellophane bag to $125.00 for elegant holiday baskets. The shop is open from 9:00 A.M. to 5:30 P.M. Monday through Saturday; call (501) 362-7919.

The town of Sugar Loaf was founded in 1882 and became Heber Springs in 1910. It's at the foot of Round Mountain and still has, downtown in Spring Park, the original spring from which it was named. Across the street from the park, the **Anderson House** is a historic country inn that has been here as long as the town—since 1882, back when this was a spa and gave Hot Springs a run for its money. Recently Larry and Sandy Anderson bought and refurbished the old inn, which now has sixteen rooms. The white, Williamsburg-type inn with its green shutters and tin roof (Larry says it's an interesting phenomenon that

Anderson House

when it rains, everyone sleeps late) has beautiful rooms and large
private bathrooms. Every other room was halved and made into
large baths with showers and deep old tubs.

The inn's bedrooms open onto a wide front porch and upper
balcony overlooking the tree-filled park. The rooms are furnished
with country antiques, mostly oak with iron beds modernized to
queen-size, each bed covered with a hand-stitched quilt made by
Larry's mom. Lace curtains and pretty wallpaper give the place a
turn-of-the-century feel. Breakfast of homemade coffeecake,
muffins, and egg casserole is served buffet-style in the large parlor, which has a tall stone fireplace and hardwood floors. The inn,
located at 201 East Main, prices its rooms at $48 to $52. Call
(501) 362–5266 for reservations.

Captains' House is a restaurant in a circa 1915 house at 603 West Quitman Street, only a half-block off Highway 25 South. A life-size mermaid greets visitors in the front hall. The restaurant's four rooms are done in a Victorian ship motif complete with Oriental rugs. Owners Beth and Jerry Nordquist recently purchased the restaurant where Jerry had been the chef for several years. Jerry specializes in healthy, low-fat dishes that emphasize the use of Arkansas products. Fresh fruit join dishes like sesame-sautéed catfish or poached catfish—dishes unique in a state where catfish is usually deep-fried. The luncheon menu has sandwiches (including a grape- and celery-filled chicken salad) that come with a salad or the soup du jour. But this is no tearoom. The menu offers foods served at a captain's table—including steak and French fries. And the devastating desserts would please any sailor's palate: fresh fruit cobblers, European torts with fresh raspberries, lemon *vacherin* (a baked meringue) with mousse. Lunch is served Monday through Saturday from 11:00 A.M. to 2:00 P.M. Dinner is served on Friday and Saturday from 5:00 to 8:00 P.M. (or until 10:00 P.M. in the summertime). Call (501) 362–3963.

Ann's Attic Crafts, at 1207 West Main, draws from 240 local craftspersons in a 20-mile radius. The shop has some unusual crafts—weavings of pine needles (tiny, tiny baskets), along with wheat weavings, Old World Santas, and hand-carved spools. Call (501) 362–2332.

There are a couple of routes around Greers Ferry Lake by highway to the towns on the other side. Sugar Loaf Mountain is between Heber Springs and the town of Greers Ferry, too, but you need a boat to get to the mountain because it rises 560 feet in the middle of Greers Ferry Lake. The first National Nature Trail established by Congress climbs to the 1,001-foot summit. The trail is an easy climb and has spectacular bird's-eye views of the lake. (There is another Sugar Loaf Mountain, a landlocked mountain that shares its name with the one in Greers Ferry Lake. It is on Highway 110 and also has a foot trail to the summit for great views.)

The drive from Heber to Fairfield Bay on Highway 16 is more scenic than the drive on Highway 92 is. If you drive through Fairfield Bay, take the time to see the arts and crafts shop at the Lakewood Village Mall. It's staffed by volunteers from the bay and is filled with needlework, paper quilling, wooden puzzles, sketches, watercolors, and hand-smocked christening gowns, to name a few items, all done by local people and all at very reasonable prices.

If you're hungry and it's feeding time, swing east on Highway 16 from Greers Ferry to the **B & G Bakery and Pizza** on Highway 9 in downtown Shirley—a little town full of friendly people and offering an old hardware store complete with potbellied stove. The bakery is the pride and joy of Bea and George Macke, who turn out warm Danish pastries every morning. Local people have their own mugs hanging on the wall (a good sign in any cafe) and sit at two long tables running the length of the room. The homemade pizza is great, too, an unexpected find in a little cafe like this one. It's thickly loaded with your favorite toppings to take home hot or eat there. Quilts, made by local women, are for sale in the cafe. Hours are from 7:00 A.M. to 7:00 P.M. Wednesday though Saturday. Call (501) 723–8185 to have a pizza waiting for you.

Now to walk off that Danish, head for the Historic Railroad Trail, a 2-mile-round-trip excursion that starts at Highway 9 at the B & G Bakery and runs along the historic Missouri and North Arkansas Railway. It goes by an Indian burial ground, and the end of the trail is at the old pioneer Cottrell-Wilson Cemetery.

Following Highway 16 west will lead to Clinton, the home of **Pentacle Studio,** a good-size gallery of fine arts, crafts, and gifts featuring stained glass by owner Roberta Katz and a phantasmagoric family of sculptures, carvings, and weavings. The Gallery of Arkansas Art proudly shows the works of more than seventy-five of Arkansas's finest artists and artisans: Alice Miller's bone and antler mobiles, Jean Shepard's wool, Doug Johnson's kaleidoscopes of stained glass and marbles, Jim Good's wooden fishing lures, and a ton of other unusual crafts. Roberta has only high-quality crafts in this gallery, and the list includes jewelry by Skip Cluff and handwoven garments (wearable art, according to Roberta) by Arlone Wonderlin-Folker. The price tags on items in the bright yellow house, which sits beneath big shade trees on the crest of a hill, range from small pieces of Mary Lou Kosmeder's colored porcelain pottery at $5.00 to a hand-carved walnut rocker by Stowe for $850 and everything in between. The shop is on Highway 65 (501–745–4589) and is open from 10:00 A.M. to 5:00 P.M. Monday through Saturday.

South of Clinton on Highway 65 in Choctaw, **Choctaw General Store** has seven rooms—10,000 square feet—of new stuff, old stuff, and stacks of rolled carpets. Antiques, old clocks by the dozens, boxes of old silver, furniture of all kinds, and stained glass windows leaning against the walls make it an adventure to wander around in Gerald and Kathleen Coogan's spacious store. The store is open from 9:00 A.M. to 5:00 P.M. daily, but since the Coogans live here it often stays open late in the summer. You can call (501) 745–2007 to check on the times.

The **Traditions Coffee Shop and Arts and Crafts,** serving devilishly good carrot cake and white-chocolate cheesecake, along with flavored and special-blend coffees and cappuccino, waits for you on Highway 65/9. It is all in a sunny little room next to a small gallery of decorative arts and canvas art in Choctaw. It is a pretty place in which to get comfortable and unwind a bit while enjoying the special creations, both culinary and artistic. Owners Carol Hempel and ElFriede Bower bring crafts in from around the area—everything from oil paintings to pendulum clocks. Carol or ElFriede know the area well and can direct you to other interesting places, too. The establishment is open from 9:00 A.M. to 5:00 P.M. daily except Wednesday. Call (501) 745–8727.

Going north from Clinton on Highway 65 leads to places tucked out of sight (the backcountry keeps its secrets to itself unless you are in a canoe) or in plain view on the highway. The highway passes the **Antiques Warehouse** in Botkinburg, one of the largest antiques shops in the Ozarks and perhaps in the state, at Highway 65/110, and it's open seven days a week. Owner Don Keathley buys and restores European furniture, all of excellent quality and ready for the finest home. The back rooms also have unrestored pieces to browse among. Along with the furniture, decorator items of brass and silver, mirrors, and hundreds of stained glass windows are there, too, and everything in the three warehouses and two showrooms dates from the 1860s to the 1880s. The telephone number at the warehouse is (501) 745–5842.

Like so many small towns across the country, Leslie fell on hard times when the railroads moved on. This was the end of the "Dinky Line," the railroad that hooked up to the Missouri and North Arkansas Railroad. The rail line was used to "logout the hollers" around here, carrying lumber to the mills. When that industry faded, the town faded, too, in spite of the proud rock homes. The seven hotels mysteriously burned, one at a time, and

Leslie went from being one of the biggest towns in northwest Arkansas to a shadow of its former self. Then longtime residents of Leslie donated money to help refurbish the town. Now the town is jumping again, and the Carousel Ice Cream Soda Fountain on Oak Street and the Leslie Cafe serve good food to visitors, who come here for the Ozark Heritage Arts Center performances done by the local theater group.

Diana Brodie, one of the theater group members, is a fascinating musician and songwriter who now has a shop in Leslie called **Designs in Metal,** where she makes hand-forged copper, silver, and bronze jewelry using an oxyacetylene torch ("like a blacksmith, only on a smaller scale"). Diana also makes marionettes, and these are her real love. The puppets are made of basswood, with papier-mâché heads. The feet and hands are black oak, and all the costumes are hand-stitched; metal parts are forged with Diana's jewelry. The prices of these collectors' items range from $300 to $1,000. Each piece of jewelry and each marionette are one of a kind, and if you call ahead (501–447–2954), you can watch Diana work. Located at 211 Oak Street, the tiny storefront shop, with its Old West or New Orleans balcony, is easy to spot.

Continue north on Highway 65 to Marshall. Northeast from Marshall on Highway 27, about 4 miles east of Harriet on Highway 14 and then north on Pole Cat Road, is the large **Big Creek (MB) Ranch**—more than 500 acres of rugged and spectacular scenery with secluded cottages tucked among the trees. Ride horses to see streams, waterfalls, bluffs, ponds, and natural springs, even an old-fashioned swimming hole on a crystal-clear creek. The large ranch is fine for folks who want to get away to a peaceful wilderness setting but still have some of the comforts of home, like a fireplace and grill (but no radio, television, or telephone). All you need to bring is food and your toothbrush and you can truly leave the world behind for a while.

Owner Frank Minirth and his wife, Mary Alice, have managed to combine the exterior wilderness and the interior fine decor into a neat hideaway. Whippoorwills sing outside the window; the sound of the creek soothes away cares. During spring there's a canoe for the creek, and year-round foreman Larry Reece and his family care for the horses and the guests. There are five cottages and two lodges, with prices starting from $89 for two persons, plus a $12 charge for each additional person. These facilities are a quarter-mile apart and are visually isolated from one another;

each has its own view. Call the foreman's house at (501) 448–5058 for reservations.

The Buffalo National River flows under Highway 65 north of Marshall, and the Tyler Bend Recreation Area follows the river. Gilbert, on Highway 333, is a gathering place for canoers paddling the river. With its 1901 saloon-style front, the **Gilbert General Store** is the same now as then. Well, maybe not *exactly* the same—in 1906 the owner added onto it a bit. But the town post office is still in a front corner, and the potbellied stove, circled by rocking chairs, still makes a warm spot for the locals to gather. The store is the heart of this quaint town on the banks of the Buffalo River, where the population can swell from 43 to 543 on any summer day. Managers Ben and Cynthia Fruehauf have been here since the 1970s and can not only provide you with anything you need in the way of canoe gear but also tell you how to find all the secret waterfalls and cliffside swimming holes. The store is open from 8:00 A.M. to 6:00 P.M. daily during the season, which runs from about March through October. Ben says they "shorten up the hours in the winter," which might mean it's closed entirely, but you never know unless you call (501) 439–2888 or 439–2386. Take Highway 65 to State Road 333; then go east on Highway 333 to the end of the road.

Tyler Bend Recreation Area has handsome camping facilities and a 6.5-mile-long hiking trail at the put-in point just off Highway 65 at the Buffalo National River. The trail creates foot access to some of the best scenery along the river—high bluffs, long sandbars, and fast water shoals. Most of the walk is along easy grades, but more difficult stretches occur along the ridgelines, where the vistas of Calf Creek are worth the effort. The trail is a series of loops adjoining one another and varying from just under 2 miles to nearly 4 miles. A 1,000-foot-long stone wall built during pioneer days and a 1930s log homestead are also found along the trail.

North of Tyler Bend on Highway 65, Coursey's Smoked Meats in St. Joe has been smoking bacon and hams for forty-five years. The place has the original old smoker out front, but now it's all done inside in stainless steel smokers. Jack Coursey is the owner, Mary Lu Coursey Neal is the manager, and they still make the best smoked bacon in the state. If you don't believe it, call (501) 439–2530 and order some.

Scenic Highway 7 is just that, one of the loveliest drives in the state. It winds and curves and crests hills and skirts rivers. It is more than just a way to get somewhere in Arkansas, and there are some great little places along the way. **Brambly Hedge Cottage Bed and Breakfast,** 4 miles south of Jasper, the hub of this area, on Scenic Highway 7 is a historic house built around a hundred-year-old log cabin—built on Sloan Mountain before the Homestead Act in 1872. Hosts Billy and Jacquelyn Smyers have uncovered a portion of the original cabin and left it exposed on the screened porch. It was added onto in a sort of hodgepodge fashion in the 1940s and covered with stucco, giving the two-story house an English Cotswolds look. (That's where the name came from: Jacquelyn loved British author-illustrator Jill Barklem's books about mice living in the brambly hedge.) The house was mentioned in a recent issue of the *National Geographic Traveler,* although only one bedroom is for guests. This upstairs bedroom has a comfortable sitting area and a private bath (or you can use the quaint outhouse, if you prefer the feeling of the good old days).

The view from the cottage is "clear to Missouri" from the deck that overlooks the Buffalo River Valley, and a full breakfast is served there, on the screened porch, or in the country kitchen. Sometimes the house is literally in the clouds; often it overlooks clouds or mist hanging over the valley. Jacquelyn's breakfast specialty is Eggs a la Goldenrod: eggs in a cream sauce made with local smoked ham and served over toast with grated egg yolk. The room costs $55, and you can call the Smyerses at (501) 446-5849.

Bordering the Ozark National Forest and the Buffalo River Park, Lendell and Laura Reddell's Ozark Mountain Cabins, about 0.3 mile off Highway 7, 4 miles north of Jasper, offer a spectacular valley view where elk and deer graze in the pastures. Each of the three log cabins sleeps six, and each has a gorgeous 20-mile view. The cabins are built of hand-peeled logs with pine tongue-and-groove walls and fireplaces of locally collected rock inside. Central heat makes the cabins a great place for winter vacations. The kitchens have everything you need; just bring food and drink. The cabins are about 150 feet apart, placed for the view, and with summer foliage they are hidden from one another. Summer rates are $70.00 for two people, plus $10.00 per additional person, ($5.00 for kids under twelve), and reduced rates are offered for stays of more than four nights; winter rates are quite a bit less. Call for reservations at (501) 446-2229.

South of Jasper on Highway 327 is Parthenon, nearby which Gloria and Jimmy Justice have created an elegant hideaway.

When you drive up to it, it looks a little ramshackle, but you're in for a surprise when you go inside, for this is **A Cabin in the Woods** with a difference. The cabin is about a half-mile from the Justices' place and furnished with its own original antiques and hardwood floors. Everything you could want is there—dishes, appliances (a microwave), and a very unexpected treat: a cedar sauna off the bathroom and a Jacuzzi on the deck. The bedrooms are in three lofts with steep stairways (not quite ladders). The cabin is rented to one party at a time, so it is ideal for anyone from honeymooners (who'll find a chilled bottle of champagne awaiting them) to folks having a family reunion; it sleeps up to ten people. There is no telephone, and the television doesn't get any stations in this remote area, but a VCR is hooked up if you want to bring your own movies. The cabin costs $60.00 for two people, plus $7.50 extra for each additional adult and $5.00 extra per child. Call the Justices at (501) 446–2293 when you reach Parthenon, and they'll lead you 2.5 miles on a dirt road to their 200-acre property with its view of the Boston Mountains.

Six miles south of Jasper on Scenic Highway 7, Ellen and Gene Pendergraft have sixty acres near the "Arkansas Grand Canyon" and operate Pendergraft Ozark Crafts in a restored 1800s log cabin. It's open daily April 1 through Thanksgiving weekend, and you can find every kind of craft imaginable. Everything comes from artists within 50 miles of the shop. Pottery, ironwork, stuffed animals, dolls, wood-carving—the list goes on. Gene's studio is just 900 feet away on the property, and there he has a gallery of his watercolors, ink drawings, and acrylics. You can usually find him there in the winter if you call ahead. Hours at the shop are from 9:30 A.M. to 5:30 P.M. You can reach Gene at (501) 446–5267 most of the year.

The Buffalo National River rushes from Ponca to the White River. This most scenic stretch of the river is floatable only in the spring, because once summer arrives it becomes a series of quiet pools. But when it runs, it runs, and it has plenty of roller-coaster rapids to enliven the scenery.

A different kind of ride will let you float silently over the Ozark Mountains in the wicker gondola of a hot-air balloon. **The Champagne Flight,** leaving the Buffalo Outdoor Center in Ponca (population 20 in winter) has this thrill for only $300 a couple (but your friends can ride in the chase vehicle with the crew if they want to). Leaving at sunrise, the flight is an hour, but with the time taken for inflation and for packing up after land-ing, it is about a three-hour adventure. Pilot and owner of the balloon Mike Mills will take you up over the mountains from the valley where Ponca is nestled. Rising above the early-morning fog to see the peaks poking above the clouds makes for a lifetime memory. And each flight is different; the wind is the navigator. Flights take place in summer and fall for the most part, with a few offered in winter (it's a bit too windy in spring). It's best to be flexible because the weather plays such an important role in hot-air ballooning.

The Buffalo Outdoor Center also has rustic log cabins for $70 each that are equipped with a full kitchen, a fireplace, loft bed-rooms, and a front porch swing. Of course, canoes, rafts, or guided johnboats for fishing trips are available, too. For further highjinks on the Buffalo River, call Steve McAdams at (501) 861–5514.

If you have never tried your hand at guiding a canoe down a river, it's never too late to begin. Doing so is not difficult, and first-time-outers often come back dry as a bone, having experi-enced no spills (but no guarantees, either). For those of you with more experience and perhaps a canoe lashed to the car, there are several put-in points in the area. If it's later in the season and the upper Buffalo is too shallow to canoe, you can put in at Woolum on the lower river, off Highway 65, and take a leisurely day trip to Silver Hill (16.5 miles), where the U.S. Park Service station is, or continue for a two-day trip (another 16 miles) to Maumee. The entire trip from Ponca takes about a week—from Woolum, about five or six days—and landings all along the river are about 4 to 20 miles apart. Canoe outfitters will pick you up where you plan to end.

The Buffalo Outdoor Center rents housekeeping cabins at Silver Hill, too; call (501) 439–2244 at Silver Hill. Canoes rent for about $25 each, and transportation to and from put-in and takeout is about $15. The Buffalo River Tower at Silver Hill offers a spectacu-lar view of five Ozark counties and the Buffalo River watershed.

Ozark National Forest

Northwest of Ponca on Highway 27 at Kingston, Wisty Rorabacher makes multilayered wooden puzzles in her home for and about children called **Images of Childhood.** These puzzles are made of birch and come in one, two, and three layers. For example, a puzzle of a tree, when removed, will have another puzzle of children in a tree house, then squirrels and birds underneath that. The puzzles are designed for children ages two to nine. Wisty and her partner, Judy Coulter, focus on scenes about children: a school bus on one layer; kids with school gear on the next. They are interracial and nonsexist and show physically challenged children acting in them. Single-layer puzzles are $9.00; double-layer, $17.95; and three-layer, $22.00. The silk-screen paints are nontoxic, water-based paints, and so the colors are not brilliant, but what they lack in brightness they make up for in number, some puzzles having more than ten colors.

Wisty's place is *really* off the beaten path. It will take you about thirty minutes of dirt-road driving to find it, but your journey will be worth the effort to see these unusual gifts. Weekends are the best time to visit, and it's wise to call ahead for directions: (501) 665–2179.

Due north of Kingston on Highway 21, Berryville's lovely old homes date back to the city's beginning. The town has a charming turn-of-the-century town square with a tree-shaded park, old-fashioned street lamps, and benches. There's a real five-and-ten, together with shops, restaurants, and museums, and a vintage drugstore still has a soda fountain. The Heritage Center on the square contains a museum whose living history displays include a schoolroom, barbershop, and moonshine still. Moreover a working village blacksmith shop shows you how tools were forged into the 1800s; Pioneer Park features vintage log cabins and an early jail; and a restored pump station houses the city's tourist information center.

The volunteers at the center will direct you to the **Saunders Memorial Museum** at 113–115 Madison. The museum has Pancho Villa's lavishly decorated .45 Colt—its right grip burned brown from the Mexican sun and its handle inset with gold, jewels, and a Mexican gold coin and nameplate. The guns of Jesse James, Billy the Kid, Annie Oakley, and Wild Bill Hickok are all part of the finest gun collection in the nation. But even if you're not a gun collector, there are many other novel items in the museum, which was a bequest to the town from the late Colonel C. Burton Saunders. Among the things to see are a tent, hand-embroidered with gold thread (made by a sheikh's 200 wives); a war bonnet and battle jacket owned by Sitting Bull (and his totem scalps); and displays of antique furniture and Native American artifacts. Mrs. Saunder's closet is there, too, with clothes and accessories, circa 1910, as well as vases, rugs, lacework, and silverware. The museum is open from March 16 to November 1. Hours are 9:00 A.M. to 5:00 P.M. every day; you can call (501) 423–2073.

The long, redwood **Currey Studio-Gallery** is between Berryville and Eureka Springs on Highway 62, 5 miles west of Berryville. Displayed are the primitive watercolor and oil paintings of Grandma Fran (Frances Currey Brown), who works in the studio. She grew up on a farm in the time of coal-oil lamps. She cooked on a wood stove and milked cows, and these images stayed with her. She began her career quite by accident, sending small drawings to a granddaughter. Since that time her brightly colored, simple paintings of country life have been recognized in books and magazines and appeared in a large number of galleries, including the International Center of Contemporary Art in Paris and the Mykonos Folklore Museum in Greece. Grandma Fran is there year-round from 8:00 A.M. to 6:00 P.M. every day of the week except Sunday, when the gallery opens at 1:00 P.M. Call Grandma Fran at (501) 423–2073.

Highway 62 weaves from Berryville to **Eureka Springs,** which is not exactly off the beaten path. Yes, you have to look closely on the map to see it, but it is the state's premier tourist town and a must-see for any Arkansas traveler. Shops and B & Bs come and go like cottonwood fluff in the breeze. Every year there are new and different places to see. There are some old standbys that would be a shame to miss and several small spots you might overlook. There are old hotels, guest cottages, tons of antiques shops, myriad art galleries, and a batch of peculiar museums (featuring bells, frogs, bibles, musical instruments, or birds).

You'll also find a profusion of restaurants with food as diverse as the "Nouveau 'Zarks" cuisine at the Dairy Hollow House (with a $30 set price) and the breaded pecan snapper at Cafe Armagost. The Victorian Sampler Tea Room (the most beautiful place in town) and Bubba's Barbecue ("It doesn't look famous, but it is") vie with a French restaurant (the Plaza) and a Czech-German restaurant (the Bavarian Inn) for your dinnertime dollar. From the most expensive (the Plaza, with a great wine list and dishes like duck with Grand Marnier sauce) to the best bargains (Chelsea's—the most food for the least money—don't be put off by just looking in the door; go on in and order the "Macho Nachos," covered with black beans, sausage, and alfalfa sprouts, and live a little) to places like the Oasis (mostly vegetarian food) and DeVitto's downtown (homemade pasta and bread and fresh trout worth the restaurant's long wait to get in) or Ermilio's (in an old house uphill on the Highway 62 loop; also Italian but very different from DeVitto's), you can find whatever you want at mealtime. The hours vary with the season, and many places are closed in winter, so check around.

The many-tiered, sprawling Victorian village dates back to 1879 on the rugged, hilly terrain of the Ozark Mountains. Today because of the collective restoration of the town, Eureka Springs offers a microcosm of late-nineteenth-century life, making it a unique, historic tourist attraction. The streets are so steep that the entrance to St. Elizabeth's Catholic Church is through the top of the bell tower, and a motorized trolley roams the town's narrow streets, none of which intersect at right angles. The trolley follows the Highway 62 loop around town with a spiderweb of tiny cul-de-sacs weaving off from it in all directions.

More than 600 artisans live and work in the Eureka Springs area, and their crafts are sold all over town. You can find quilts, knives, baskets, Quaker furniture, stained glass—almost anything—here. The shops are crammed with fine arts and oddities. The first thing to do is park your car and buy a trolley ticket. The streets are impossibly narrow, and there is never a parking meter vacant. You can get off and on the trolley as much as you want to and see a lot more that way. (The secret is to ride it *twice* up hill and walk down, riding on the right side the first time and the left side the second time.)

A free walking tour leaves from in front of the New Orleans Hotel every Sunday and is led by gray-haired Virginia Tyler, who has lived here since she was eight years old. The tour leaves about 7:15 A.M. in the warm summer months and about 1:15 P.M. in the fall. Or you can get a walking-tour book for under $2.00 from the Chamber of Commerce.

Singleton House B & B is a pretty, 2-story Victorian at 11 Singleton Street. Innkeeper Barbara Gavron also has a service listing more than thirty B & Bs and cottages in the area. Barbara tries to match people up with the kind of place they want. She knows every street and path and is a gold mine of information. (She likes to send her guests out at night with a flashlight to see the beauty of the town after dark; go to the top of the old hotels and get romantic night views, she says.)

The Singleton House has five bedrooms, three of which have private baths. A breakfast balcony overlooks the garden and pond out behind the kitchen. A full breakfast (spinach quiche, fresh fruit) is included in the $65 to $75 price. A Sunday hiking club leaves from here, too. The phone number for Barbara's reservation service and the Singleton House is (501) 253–9111.

Singleton Street is one of the web of streets winding off of the main loop. A larger main street, Spring Street, is shaded by sycamores, colored with spring daffodils and irises, and lined with B & Bs and shops. The springs still flow from the bluffs that line the street, and a new copper-topped gazebo was recently added near one of them. Bob and Betty Cowie of Cowie Wineries have recently purchased the Spring Street House Restaurant at 124 Spring Street (right by the trolley stop). The regional cooking is done on the light side and features chicken and fish and crisply cooked fresh vegetables. But the restaurant also has the best filet around and wonderfully rich desserts (ask for Jennifer's Temptation if you like chocolate). The wine list has a good selection, including the Cowies' own Arkansas wines. Call (501) 253–8558 for reservations because Spring Street House, like so many other restaurants in town, is very busy during the season.

Across the street from the restaurant, at 123 Spring, is the Uptown Pottery Shop, and down below, at 127½ Spring, is Uncle Shelby's Gentlemen's Antiques, a shop specializing in men's antique accessories—hats, razors, old footballs, and cufflinks. It's a neat little shop you might miss because the sign out front simply says ANTIQUES.

As the name implies, Eureka Springs was once a spa. The Palace Hotel and Bathhouse, at 135 Spring Street, is a restored Victorian hotel that has the only bathhouse in town and a staff of licensed therapists. Ask for "the works" and get a mineral bath, steam bath, clay mask, and thirty-minute massage for $35. The eight hotel suites contain king-size beds; a bar, sink, and refrigerator; and a whirlpool unit to modernize the comfort of the antique furniture. A continental breakfast of juice, coffee, and pastries and an evening snack tray are included in the $85 to $100 price. Call (501) 253–7474 for an appointment or a room.

Two major fires occurred in town in 1871 and 1880. The building code was changed, and the walls are now 18 inches of solid rock between the buildings, which all have tin roofs. That's why a place like **Harp's Grocery Store,** at 63 North Main and the oldest business in town, is still standing across the street from the stone steps that once led to a hotel burned to the ground in a later fire. Zoe and Albert Harp are at their store every day from 8:00 A.M. until 6:00 or 7:00 P.M. and have been for forty years. They are eighty-seven years old and have been married for sixty-seven years, and the store has never been closed a day in 106 years, even when the hotel across the street was a holocaust of flames.

"Where y'all from?" is the first question Albert asks the hundreds of strangers who pass through the store. "We are the only native people left in town," Zoe says pensively, and she'll go on to tell you she went to Carrie Nation's Sunday school; her dad was the chief of police who tried to keep Carrie out of swinging-door saloons because such an establishment "wasn't anyplace for a lady" to wield her hatchet. Their son Joe, a World War II pilot, opened a pawnshop next door to help people buy groceries in hard times, and Zoe's doll museum is in the next building ($1.00 to see the finest doll collection anywhere). Buy a bottle of sarsaparilla and listen to the stories the Harps have to tell about the grocery store, whose shelves are lined with old iron toys, ancient calendars, old photographs, dolls, and a few groceries. Someone recently offered the couple $200,000 for the contents of the store, and the Harps just wondered why anyone would think they wanted to sell it.

Stone fences, old farmhouses, and creeks make a lovely drive along Highway 187 north of Eureka Springs. If you want to take a nostalgic drive across one of the last single-lane swinging bridges left, take Highway 187 northwest toward Holiday Island to the town of Beaver. You can also reach the bridge by driving 4.5 miles back from the Highway 62/187 junction after you have visited these interesting places:

Outside of Eureka Springs on Highway 62 West, down a wooded trail, stands **Thorncrown Chapel,** a tall and glittering glass chapel tucked into the Ozarks woods. In May, when the spring canopy of leaves hasn't yet eclipsed the light, wildflowers carpet the forest floor. It is a peaceful spot, dedicated to God by a dreamer named Jim Reed and his wife, Dell, who found E. Fay Jones, a nationally honored and recognized architect, to design the chapel of glass and two-by-fours that sits on eight acres of

Harp's General Store

woods. The chapel, surrounded by blue sky and filled with sunlight, is just 60 feet long, 24 feet wide, and 48 feet tall, with eleven rows of bench seats. It holds only about a hundred people.

The base was made from the roughly cut sandstone of the surrounding hills. To avoid using building materials too large to carry down the path, cross-braced, hand-rubbed timbers 2 by 4 feet and 2 by 6 feet and infilled with glass were used. The more than 6,000 square feet of glass in the walls and central skylight reflect the sunlight in patterns that change with the time and the seasons and let the chapel blend into surrounding timber as though it had grown there. It is called "Ozark Gothic"—Gothic in reverse, in that darkness becomes light. The chapel has seasonal hours: daily 9:00 A.M. to 6:00 P.M. April through October; until 5:00 P.M. in November; and 11:00 A.M. to 4:00 P.M. December through March. It is closed in January and February. Sunday services are at 9:00 and 11:00 A.M., with a special 7:00 A.M. service from June through October. The church is nondenominational, and the Reverend Doug Reed, son of the founders, is minister. Call (501) 253–7401 for information.

The area around Eureka has been an artists' colony since the 1930s and is a fine arts center. Galleries are everywhere. Hundreds of artists live and work in the area. The Inspiration Point Fine Arts Colony on Highway 62 has a summer opera workshop, with opera performances from mid-June to mid-July (one young singer calls it "the boot camp of opera"), and sponsors a barbershop quartet weekend, as well as blues and jazz festivals.

At the junction of Highways 62 and 37 at Gateway, you'll see the Hillbilly Eatin' Place and Dari Bar ("Vittles to go"). Although the place is not much to look at, inside you'll find homemade strawberry rhubarb, peanut butter, and cherry cheesecake pies and the most magnificent pork tenderloin and potato wedges available anywhere. Hours are from 6:00 A.M. (7:00 A.M. on Sunday) for homemade cinnamon rolls to 8:00 P.M. for the daily specials, which are down-home good things like homemade chicken and noodles or fried chicken.

Off Highway 62 north of Rogers, the National Park Service has rebuilt the historic Elkhorn Tavern on the eastern overlook of Pea Ridge Battlefield (giving a good view of the western portion of the battlefield) and has fixed up the battle site with a visitors' center for history buffs. A taped slide show and lecture every half-hour and a walk-through museum or a drive-through tour (accompanied by recorded messages) of the battlefield make it possible for visitors to get both the Yankee and the Rebel perspectives on one of the only major battles fought in the state but the battle that saved Missouri for the Union.

The second of architect E. Fay Jones's crystal chapels is in Bella Vista. It is a nondenominational chapel just off of Highway 340, east of Highway 71. The Mildred B. Cooper Memorial Chapel has similar dimensions to those of the Thorncrown Chapel, 24 feet by 65 feet and 50 feet high, but this chapel uses steel, whereas Thorncrown is made of wood. The dominant pattern is curved, like a Gothic arch, rather than triangular, as is Thorncrown. It is open from 9:00 A.M. to 5:00 P.M. seven days a week; call (501) 855–6598 for more information.

Down Highway 71 from Bella Vista, Bentonville's town square has what looks like a 1950s five-and-dime—it even has a red and white awning—but the new **Wal-Mart Visitors Center** occupies the spot where Sam and Helen Walton, Arkansas natives, opened the first Walton five-and-dime, a Ben Franklin store at 105 North Main. The inside is different, though. It traces the phenomenal growth of the giant discount store chain—today's general store—from its beginning right through the year 2000. There are relics from such companies as Procter and Gamble, Johnson and Johnson, and Kimberly-Clark. This is a real "local boy makes good" story. The center is open from 9:00 A.M. to 5:00 P.M. Monday through Saturday; call (501) 273–1329.

The **Antique and Art Gallery** is next door, at 101 North Main in the old Terry-Block Building, which has not changed a bit inside. Steve Whysel and Shana Miner Whysel carry fine antiques. The shop is filled with art glass, art pottery, porcelain, Oriental rugs, and antique art. Oils, watercolors, and prints in heavy frames line the walls. Bookcases with antiquarian books richly bound in leather await collectors. But what makes this shop special is Steve's expertise in art nouveau lamps, the field in which he is the adviser to *Schroeder's Antiques Price Guide*. Steve restores antique lamps and makes lamps from antique lamp parts. Many are topped with custom-made, reproduction fringed shades, but whenever possible Steve hunts out the old glass shade the lamp may have had originally. The result is an elegant lamp of brass, pewter, or crystal to complement any decor. The shop's hours are Monday through Saturday from 10:00 A.M. to 5:00 P.M. Steve can be reached at (501) 273–7770.

The square is the hub of the town, of course, and every other weekend beginning in April there is a farmers' market on the square where you can pick your favorite fresh produce and enjoy the camaraderie of the townsfolk at The Filling Station, a cafe on the square where most everyone passes through at one time or another. This is a clean, lovely town, with many well-kept old houses. It is also the home of the annual Phillips Celebrity Golf Classic.

If you stay on Highway 71, you will be in the Rogers area. And no, **Rogers** wasn't named for Will Rogers, although Will Rogers was married to a local girl (Betty Blake) here in 1906. The Victorian 1895 Hawkins House at 322 South Second Street is now the Rogers Historical Museum, and guides will give you a taste of the history of the area with old photos, handmade furnishings, and forgotten tools. A barbershop, bank, and dry goods store are assembled in great detail right down to the clipped hair on the floor by the broom. The "Attic" is stocked with antique toys, clothes, and tools to explore. Rogers was a boomtown in the 1880s, when the railroad established a depot and apple orchards began to be planted; this was called the "Land of the Big Red Apple." A red Frisco caboose is parked 4 blocks from the museum for children to climb aboard. Hours are from 10:00 A.M. to 4:00 P.M. Tuesday through Saturday; call (501) 621–1154.

If you want the real thing, though, board the **Boston Mountains Rail Excursion Company**'s restored, five-car vintage train at Rogers's Frisco Depot and see the mountains, Winslow Tunnel, and the countryside in a way you've never seen it. The three-hour Northern Excursion to Exeter runs on the first, third, and fifth Saturdays of each month. The Southern Excursion, on the second and fourth Saturdays, goes to Fayetteville and Winslow Tunnel for a three-and-a-half-hour trip. The train carries 250 passengers and leaves from Rogers at 11:25 A.M. every Saturday (boarding is at 10:45 A.M.). First-class fare, which includes complimentary snacks and soft drinks, in the dome car is $35.00, and dinner is $8.97 in the first-class dining car. Standard coach fare is $24.00 (for children under 12, $17.50), and dinner is $6.97. Call the Rogers Chamber of Commerce at (800) 364–1240 or (501) 636–1240 for information.

Downtown Rogers has been restored to what it was when the town was young. Go through the 9-foot-tall doors decorated with bas-relief sculptures of mortar and pestle and into Poor Richard's at 116 South First Street. It is as it was as a pharmacy both inside and out. Oak woodwork, glass shelves, and a marble soda fountain are accented with wrought iron tables and chairs—a fine place for a big chocolate soda on a hot day. The building was constructed of marble from nearby Carthage, Missouri. The shop contains solid mahogany fixtures, and the marble soda fountain has a mahogany back bar and room divider that offers a fine example of the cabinetmaker's craft of the time. A large mahogany clock with brass movement hangs on the wall to your left as you enter the store; its enamel face has kept time since 1907. The tile floor and pressed-tin ceiling tiles are original. The porcelain drawer pulls are inscribed with the names of the various drugs—in Latin—and pharmaceutical supplies. The store is open Monday through Saturday from 9:30 A.M. to 6:00 P.M. and is especially delightful during the Christmas season, when carolers are on hand and the store is decorated in holiday sparkles and open later. Call (501) 631–7687 for information.

At First and Elm streets, around the block from Poor Richard's in a blue-and-white-trimmed building, is The Crumpet Tea Room. Lunch in this second-floor restaurant is from 11:00 A.M. to 2:00 P.M. Monday through Saturday. Good things like quiche join unusual things like the "crumpet potatoe," baked with vegetables and sauce, and the tearoom's famous hot orange rolls with orange frosting. Desserts? You betcha—chocolate pie and cheesecake. Call (501) 636–7498 for other daily specials.

Arkansas Discovery Bed and Breakfast is the name of the two-story, brick and white country home at 1801 Highway 12 East in Rogers. Built as a B & B by Kay and Ted Solarz, the house is close to Beaver Lake and nestled among oak, dogwood, and redbud trees on a ridge of the Ozark Mountains. The four guest rooms are furnished country-style, and the fireplace in the living room is a fine spot to gather on chilly autumn evenings. The downstairs bedrooms have private baths, the two upstairs rooms share a connecting bath, and the $54 price includes a full breakfast with fresh fruit and such inviting entrees as peach pancakes, French toast, or oven omelets, served with sausage, bacon, or ham. Breakfast can be enjoyed in the dining room or, in good weather, on the veranda. Call (501) 925–1744 for reservations.

If you want to try a hickory-smoked ham done in the Ozark tradition—slowly, over natural hickory smoke, using an old family recipe dating back to 1841—then stop by Hillbilly Smokehouse (501–636–1927) at 1801 South Eighth Street (Highway 71B South) for sugar or salt dry-cured ham and bacon. The secret is slow curing and aging, which create the delightful taste and texture. Hours are Monday through Wednesday 6:00 A.M. to 6:00 P.M., Thursday and Friday until 8:00 P.M., and Saturday until 4:00 P.M. Call 800–759–9439 for a catalog of other meats available—turkey, sausage, and chicken.

War Eagle, south of Rogers on Highway 12, is the site of the huge War Eagle Fair, a four-day event that brings thousands of visitors each May and October to see handmade, one-of-a-kind Ozarks crafts in tents covering acres of ground. The fair always begins on the first Friday in May and the third Thursday in October. Across a one-lane rusty steel bridge (with a TWO-TON-LIMIT sign), the War Eagle Mill Arts and Crafts Fair competes on the mill side of the river, and what seems to be more than two tons of traffic and pedestrians flow back and forth. You can reach the fair from the south on Highway 303 for easier (and free) parking.

War Eagle Mill is a reproduction of an 1873 gristmill powered by the War Eagle River with three sets of stone buhrs and an 18-foot redwood undershot waterwheel. First built in 1830, the mill washed away in 1848. The second mill was burned by order of a Confederate general to prevent the Union army's use of it. This undershot waterwheel is the only one of its kind operating. Inside is War Eagle Mercantile, an old-fashioned general store with all manner of jams, honey, herbs, mixes, rugs, toys, clothing, pottery, and dozens of other things. The working water-powered gristmill is still making stone-buhr-ground cornmeal, whole wheat flour, rye, and yellow corn grits.

In the same building The Bean Place Lunchroom serves War Eagle buckwheat waffles and biscuits and sausage gravy for breakfast; for lunch there are always beans and cornbread, smoked ham and turkey, and home-baked cakes, tarts, and cookies—all with apple cider and all made right there at the mill. The Bean Place is open seven days a week from 8:30 A.M. to 4:00 P.M. but closes January 1 until March 3. Take County Road 98 from Highway 12, or call (501) 789–5343. The mill is open seven days a week from 8:30 A.M. to 5:00 P.M., except January and February, when it is open Saturday and Sunday only.

Traveling south on Highway 71 makes it easy to detour over to Tontitown on Highway 412 West. This is an Italian community separated from nearby Fayetteville by vineyards. Settled in 1898 by Father Bandini, Tontitown was named after the first Italian to explore the state, Henri De Tonti. The neat white Tontitown Historical Museum, on Highway 68 West, features an early grape press, wine bottling, and spaghetti machines. It is open June through August on Wednesday, Saturday, and Sunday from 1:00 to 4:00 P.M.; September through October it is open Saturday and Sunday from 1:00 to 4:00 P.M. Call (501) 361–2498 for information. The museum tells the story of the settlement of the town, but to get the true feeling of the community, try to be there for the Tontitown Grape Festival, one of the state's oldest continuous festivals, featuring handmade spaghetti and sauce and at the St. Joseph Church and school that Father Bandini founded.

There are two old Italian restaurants in town. The Venesian Inn, on Highway 68–Henri de Tonti, is owned by Alice Leatherman and has been here since 1947, in the same brick building in which it began. It is always busy, but the service is immediate —the salad (just lettuce covered with a strong garlic and oil dressing that everyone seems to love) is brought right away; fresh warm bread served with honey, basic Italian fare (spaghetti or ravioli) and chicken or steak entrees follow. The restaurant is open for dinner Tuesday through Saturday; call (501) 361–2562.

The other Italian restaurant is quite different. Tablecloths, soft lighting, and a good wine list make **Mary Maestri's,** located at Highway 412 West and Maestri Road, more upscale. A more complete selection of homemade pastas and sauces, including excellent lasagna and tortellini, join Italian entrees like chicken piccata (a favorite—cooked on the grill with lemon butter), the best steaks in the region, and, of course, homemade spumoni, pies, and New York cheesecake for dessert. Owner Danny Maestri is Mary's grandson, and the restaurant and its traditions have been here for sixty-eight years, since a poor grape harvest left Aldo and Mary Maestri looking for ways to increase their income. Mary, using her mother-in-law's spaghetti sauce, opened a restaurant in their home, and the place was such a hit that more and more tables were squeezed in. At one point even the beds were used as chairs, with small tables between them, and when that wasn't enough, customers often used their laps as tables. The fried chicken and spaghetti dinner was the favorite and still is. All the spaghetti you want with any entree is still traditional, so you will never leave hungry. Hours are 5:30 to 9:30 P.M.; call (501) 361–2536.

Stay on Highway 412 west of Tontitown to the Oklahoma border, where Sugar Creek flows right through the town of Siloam Springs. The hundred-year-old town grew up around mountain springs. Restored Victorian homes and buildings dot the town, which is filled with art galleries, craft shops, and picture-book parks. It is the home of John Brown University and the Sager Creek Arts Center for the performing arts.

If you plan to spend the night in Siloam Springs, the **Washington Street Bed and Breakfast**—Ruby Lawson's large, two-and-a-half-story Victorian home—is an inviting place, set on six private acres of maple trees. Chickens hunt and peck around the yard, and fresh eggs are always on the breakfast menu; a rooster gives an early-morning wake-up call to guests. The house features a wraparound porch with a hammock and swing and is furnished with antiques. The large living room is often used for wedding receptions, and the television room and VCR are available for guests to enjoy. The two $50 rooms each have a private half-bath; the bathroom with tub and shower is shared. You'll find the B & B at 1001 South Washington Street. Call (501) 524–5669 for reservations.

Springdale is the home of Tyson Foods, and driving down Highway 71 behind trucks filled with chicken crates feels like riding in a ticker-tape parade of chicken feathers. **Johnson House Bed & Breakfast,** on Forty-eighth Street off Great House Springs Road (behind the mill), is between Springdale and Fayetteville in Johnson on Highway 71. This circa 1882 home of handmade brick features three restored bedrooms, all with private baths. Hostess Mary Carothers receives guests in the front parlor, which has a wood-burning fireplace and an intricately painted ceiling. A full breakfast, with such unusual specialties as blueberry gingerbread, apple crisp, or cheese grits, is served in the window-filled dining room, which looks out over a hillside. Guests can walk in the gardens or visit the antiques shop on the grounds. The upstairs veranda offers a beautiful sunset view. Rooms are $75, with special winter rates. Call (501) 756–1095 for reservations.

Highway 23—from Highway 16 to I–40—leads into Fayetteville and is known as "The Pig Trail" to Razorback fans who travel north through a canopy of forest toward Fayetteville for home games. Fayetteville is a city where you can wine and dine and shop till you drop and still be only minutes away from the unspoiled mountains, lakes, and streams of surrounding country. It is the home of the state's largest university, the University of Arkansas. Old Main, the most famous building on campus, rises on a hill with its massive red brick walls and mansard roof marking the campus. Its twin towers stand watch over the university campus and the Razorbacks who call it home. You can choose an atmosphere to suit your whimsy: the laid-back, anything-goes attitude on Dickson Street; the beer-and-boots cowboy scene south of downtown; several college hot spots that mix hard rock with huge dance spaces; the disco crowd on the square; and a couple of fine listening clubs for the quieter set.

If eating's your thing, you are in luck in Fayetteville. Colorful taverns and restaurants surround the campus, and there's even an old-fashioned farmers' market every Tuesday, Thursday, and Saturday morning May through October, from 7:00 A.M. to 1:00 P.M., on the vibrant town square that's alive with flowers and trees, produce and crafts. The historic district at Washington and Willow streets between Dickson and Davidson is filled with Victorian mansions and large shade trees. Tours of the district and of Headquarters House, an 1853 frame structure that served both sides during the Civil War, are included on a walking tour, along with many of the town's historic homes. A tour can be arranged through the Historical Society at Old Jail, 30 South College Street (501–521–2970).

The **Arkansas Air Museum,** located in the vast, all-wood White Hangar of Fayetteville's Drake Field on Highway 71 South, houses everything from famous racing planes of the 1920s and 1930s to an early airliner. Music of the 1940s plays in the hangar to help you drift back in time. But this is no ordinary museum; here the colorful displays take off and soar. The planes are maintained and licensed and can be seen in the air earning the name "The Museum That Flies." There are open-cockpit biplanes and closed-cabin monoplanes all up, up, and away at various times. The volunteers who open the museum from 9:30 A.M. to 4:30 P.M. daily are lifelong pilots and mechanics whose love of airplanes and sense of humor keep the hangar full of life. A free movie, *Aviation Oddities,* shows many of the bizarre contraptions people have built to try their wings. You can also watch antique airplanes being restored in the museum's restoration shop.

Admission is free, although a donation box helps fund the non-profit all-volunteer museum and a gift shop sells model airplanes and T-shirts. Call (501) 521–4947 for information.

Highway 16 between the "Pigtrail" and Fayetteville shows the beauty of the prairies and woodlands colored by the wildflowers that grow in the hollows and along the creeks. But digging these plants is not encouraged anymore, because of the delicate balance of the ecology.

The **Holland Wild Flower Farm,** at 290 O'Neal Lane in Elkins on Highway 16, is where Bob and Julie Holland have another way to fill your yard: with the reds of cardinal flowers, the blue of flocks, the purple of coneflower, or the dramatic burst of color of the orange butterfly weed. The farm offers wildflower seeds and native plants. A visit to the farm is like a nature walk, abloom with native color. The gardens and flower beds, together with the fields of wildflowers and native plants, offer wild columbines, iris, and other native perennials—all nursery propagated. Bob has a degree in wildlife research and plant pathology, Julie is a biologist, and the two have plenty of helpful advice to offer on how to raise the plants you select. The nursery and shop are open April through November on Thursday through Saturday from 9:30 A.M. to 6:00 P.M. The farm is a half-mile from Highway 16 off of First Street. Call (501) 643–2622 for a catalog ($1.50) for future orders.

The Bluebird House at Terra in Durham, also on Highway 16, is where you can find your Bluebird of Happiness, at Terra Studios, 16 miles southeast of Fayetteville. You can watch the famous little glass bluebirds being made by skilled glass craftspeople. There is a large stoneware pottery showroom, too. Rita Ward's clay-sculptured "Terrans," tiny elflike creatures who live at Terra, are popular with collectors of gnomes and such, and John Ward's unusual large urns are displayed out front. The Ward family has produced elegance everywhere. This is one of the few working family studios in the nation. It has two complete pottery studios and a 5,000-square-foot hot glass studio. The lovely grounds include a picnic area under the cedars, an arched bridge, and a garden; visitors picnic in the hand-built clay gazebo beyond the arched bridge. The facility is open seven days a week from 9:00 A.M. to 5:00 P.M.; call (501) 643–3185.

Off the Beaten Path in West Central Arkansas

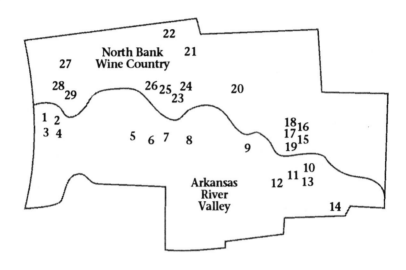

1. Patent Model Museum
2. Miss Laura's
3. Cathedral Stained Glass
4. Taliano's
5. Classic Candies
6. Cowie Winery
7. The Grapevine Restaurant
8. Subiaco Abbey
9. Mount Nebo State Park
10. Cedar Falls
11. Museum of Automobiles
12. Tanyard Springs
13. Adrienne's Restaurant
14. Heifer Project International Learning and Livestock Center
15. Potts Tavern
16. River Valley Arts Center
17. Ozark Heritage Craft Village
18. Stoby's
19. Jimmy Lile's Handmade Knives
20. Big Piney Creek
21. Shadow Lake Ranch
22. Bunkhouse Mulberry Ranch
23. Post Familie Winery
24. St. Mary's Mountain Bed and Breakfast
25. Wiederkehr Village
26. Mount Bethel Winery
27. Ozark Highlands Trail
28. Ozark Scenic Railway
28. Old Van Buren Inn Bed and Breakfast and Restaurant

West Central Arkansas

In Kansas the Arkansas River is called the Ar-KANSAS River, but when it crosses the state line it changes its name, because in 1881 the legislature appointed a committee to ascertain the right pronunciation of the word, and the result was a resolution declaring it to be ARK-an-saw.

The western Arkansas River Valley glides from Fort Smith to Little Rock and is quilted with pastures, vineyards, forests, and rice-fields. Rocky, towering mountain ranges line both sides—the Ozarks to the north, with lakes and hardwood forests, and the Ouachitas to the south, with pine forests and waterfalls.

The river crackles with life. Locks and dams divide the river into long lakes (dotted with sails, skiers, boats, and barges). A bouquet of small towns cluster around Fort Smith and lie sprinkled along the 160-mile valley with old depots, stagecoach stops, a frontier fort, and a monastery.

Scenic highways connect the towns. Highway 22 rolls east from Fort Smith to Dardanelle through farmland nestled between the river and steep slopes of the mountains. Highway 7, of course, is one of the nation's most scenic drives, wandering through both the Ozark and the Ouachita mountains from Harrison to Hot Springs.

Arkansas River Valley

When Fort Smith was founded at the confluence of the Arkansas and Poteau rivers, it was frontier America at its worst. Outlaws, bushwhackers, and gunrunners heading southwest joined gold seekers and whores. This place had it all. It was a tough boom-town known as "Hell on the Border," with a federal judge and a band of U.S. marshals who sent seventy-nine outlaws to the gallows. (Judge Isaac Parker, "The Hanging Judge," is famous for saying, "*I* never hung a man; it's the law.")

The fort was built at Belle Point on the Arkansas River in 1817, and the Butterfield stage line stopped here on its way to San Francisco. This was also the Arkansas terminus of the Trail of Tears, which sent the remnants of the five great civilized Indian tribes to the Oklahoma Territory.

The Victorian-era Belle Grove Historic District, on the banks of the Arkansas River off Rogers Avenue, dates back to the boom-town days. This charming time capsule has some of the best antiques shopping around. The Old Fort Museum, at 320 Rogers Avenue, is 1 block away and has a nostalgic Trolley Museum where two turn-of-the-century trolleys are being restored. The museum depicts the growth of the town and contains a circa 1900 pharmacy, including a working soda fountain and a steam-powered fire pump. It's open daily from 9:00 A.M. to 5:00 P.M. June through August and Tuesday through Saturday from 10:00 A.M. to 5:00 P.M., (Sunday from 1:00 to 5:00 P.M.) the rest of the year. Call (501) 783–7841 for information.

The Fort Smith Art Center, situated in the 1871 pink brick, Victorian Second Empire Vaughn-Schaap home at 423 North Sixth, was the first building restored in the Belle Grove Historic District. It displays the work of artists from around the world as well as area artists. But the home is worth a visit for itself alone. It contains a bathtub that an entire Brownie troop, twenty-nine girls, once stood in. Admission is free. Hours are from 9:30 A.M. to 4:30 P.M. Tuesday through Saturday and from 2:00 to 4:00 P.M. Sunday.

The **Patent Model Museum,** at 400 North Eighth Street in the historic district, occupies one of the older houses in the city. Built in the 1840s, it is a copy of the barracks of the second fort (on smaller scale, of course), with a wide front porch and lots of chimneys. The museum holds eighty-five working models—in miniature form, made by inventors to show how their creations would work—of inventions applying for patents from 1836 to 1870. Models of rotary engines, printing presses, refrigerators, and toys, each unique, will fascinate today's space-age generation. Carolyn Pollan purchased the house in 1973 and, with the help of an old photograph, had it restored to its original design. The office is open from 9:00 A.M. to 4:30 P.M. Monday through Friday; call (501) 782–9014.

The Clayton House, at 514 North Sixth Street in the district, is an example of Classic Revival Victorian architecture. It has been restored and refurbished in period furnishings and contains original belongings. Hours are Tuesday through Saturday from noon until 4:00 P.M. and Sunday from 1:00 to 4:00 P.M.; call (501) 783–3000. Admission is by donation.

Regina Chase has been making apple-head dolls in Fort Smith for about ten years. She travels to crafts shows and displays them in her home at 2214 North Fifty-fifth Lane. Her 1880s colonial lady, farmer, nurse, Uncle Sam, and Betsy Ross dolls are authentically dressed. But a favorite is the peddler doll, patterned after the 1840s women who went door to door selling goods, wearing a cape to cover them during the frequent London rains.

The heads are made of apples (dried in a dehydrator) that have been hand-carved, placed in silica gel, and then dipped in lacquer; the boots and hands are painted clay. Each doll is unique. Although the dolls last indefinitely, they will turn dark with age. "That's when they become collectors' items," says Regina. "A friend of mine has an eighty-year-old doll that belonged to her grandmother." Prices range from $30 to $45. Call ahead (501–783–1470) to make sure Regina is home.

Ed Walker's Drive-In is certainly not fancy—you would probably drive right by it. But it probably has the only curbside beer service in the state (maybe in the country) to go with its famous French dip or huge hamburger steak that is smothered in onions and oozing brown gravy. Pop inside and check out the baseball caps hanging from the ceiling; new ones are added daily. You'll find the eatery at 1500 Towson (501–783–3352). You can drive in from 11:00 A.M. until 10:00 P.M. Monday through Saturday.

Miss Laura's was once a bawdy Front Street "social club."

Well, it was a brothel, to be truthful.

Actually Miss Laura Zeigler ran the best whorehouse in town, they say.

Now the historic building (you bet it's historic—if walls could talk!) is a restaurant, offering great food both for those with common missionary tastes (country fried steak, catfish, ribeye) and for those with more, um, exotic tastes (veal Oscar and lobster). It is the only bordello on the National Register of Historic Places and is still cookin' Tuesday through Saturday from 5:00 P.M. Just follow B Street clear down and across to the wrong side of the railroad tracks to the river park. You can hear the lonesome whistle as the trains pass the colorful house, which sits alone by the river at North B Street and the Clayton Expressway. Call (501) 782–5456 for information.

Jean Williams has been making stained glass creations for more than thirty-two years and began his career doing commission windows for homes and churches. He and his partner of fifteen years, Ann Giffert, now create smaller items, too, in their shop, **Cathedral Stained Glass,** at 11 North Third Street in

CATHY JOHNSON

Miss Laura's

Fort Smith—sun catchers, window hangings, Tiffany-type lamps. But the kaleidoscopes are the most enchanting items; they range in size and price from a small (ten-inch) triangle of stained glass for $23 to the larger $60 scopes and are made entirely of stained glass. Marbles create the unique colors and are interchangeable to generate ever-changing images in the $26.50 scope. Other items in the shop are the popular stained glass hummingbird and a delicate display of pressed native wildflowers between clear and opaque glass with colored glass trim that sells for $22. Call the shop at (501) 785-1279.

Taliano's, at 201 North Fourteenth, was born when Tom Caldarera and Jim Cadelli, childhood friends, wanted to start a restaurant. Across the street from Caldarera's home stood an old mansion, the Sparks Mansion, built in 1887, that Caldarera had made into apartments. The mansion, shaded by grand old magnolia trees, has been reborn. The chandeliers, the stained glass, the hand-carved wooden dividers, and the rest of its original Renaissance Revival beauty were restored, and it has since been named to the National Register of Historic Places. Now the two men, whose families were from northern Italy (Jim's) and Sicily (Tom's), serve handmade pastas and sauces that reflect that heritage.

There are five dining rooms on the first floor. The original brass chandeliers have been converted to electricity, and the marble fireplaces were imported from Carrara, Italy. A white stone porch surrounding one side has been glassed in, and there white wrought iron tables and chairs also seat guests. For twenty-one years Caldarera and Cadelli have done all the cooking, at first with the help of their Italian parents, and the recipes are still the same family favorites. The pastas are all homemade, as are the sauces, of course. Even the sausages are specially made. Prices range from $6.95 for the delicious Giardinara Pasta, made with mushrooms and peppers, olive oil, and Parmesan, to $13.50 for veal dishes. Taliano's is open Monday through Saturday from 5:00 to 9:00 P.M. Call (501) 785–2292 for reservations.

Drive along Highway 22 from Fort Smith. The highway parallels I–40 along the south banks of the Arkansas River. The river valley has mountains sloping up on both sides, creating rich bottomland for small farms along the roadway, where horses graze in the fields.

The town of Ratcliff is on Highway 22, and right next to the post office Kendall and Debbie Poe of **Classic Candies** make the perfect gift to take home with you: a chocolate almond bar with the outline of the state impressed upon it. But that's not all they make: There are thirty different kinds of chocolate. And not just peanut brittle but black walnut brittle and pecan brittle, all made with molasses and butter. You can stop and watch through big windows as the Poes hand-dip clusters and turtlelike chocolates, a pecan and caramel treat. Take a price list home, and, when you run out, call (501) 635–2639 and the Poes will ship you more (but not from May through September, when the goodies would become chocolate pecan soup before they reached you).

Cowie Winery is about 3.5 miles out of Paris in Carbon City. The stone and cedar building is owned by Bob and Betty Cowie.

A great-great-uncle of the Cowie family came from Switzerland to Altus, where he spent his lifetime propagating new varieties of grapes—nine of them, to be exact. Today's bottles of Cowie wine have artist labels—pen-and-ink sketches of a ridge scene near the winery—and now an annual series with limited edition prints is available. The winery is open weekends only, from 9:00 A.M. to 6:00 P.M., but if you call ahead during the week—(501) 963–3990—Betty is often there.

Vineyards begin to appear along the roads outside of Paris. The scenery is *trés bien,* as peaceful as a day in France, and there's even an old monastery looking down from a hill. This is wine country, and wine country is the same all over the world, *n'est-ce pas?* Rolling east on Highway 22 is like a drive in the Provence region of France, with low stone walls curving beside the road.

Paris is the gateway to Mount Magazine in the Ozark National Forest, the highest point between the Rockies and the Appalachian Mountains. Hang gliders and rock climbers practice their daring sports on these great sandstone bluffs watched over by an Ozark National Forest ranger station. Dramatically rising 2,750 feet above the view, which is, of course, spectacular, the mountain lures scientists, naturalists, and explorers. Like the rest of the Ozark Mountains, this was once the vast floor of an ancient sea and is home to several rare and endangered trees, the Ozark chinquapin, the maple-leaved oak tree (not found anywhere else), and the yellowwood tree noted for the large, impressive clusters of flowers that hang from its branches in the springtime. Unlike the lush northern rim, the southern rim is dry and home to species of cacti and stunted and twisted oaks 200 years old and less than 50 feet tall.

Highway 309 leads to the top of Mount Magazine and connects with Scenic Highway 10. Blue Mountain Lake is hidden in the mountains between the Ozark and Ouachita national forests, just off Highway 10 west of Danville.

The area along the Arkansas River was settled by German Catholics, who were reminded of their homeland and had brought along winemaking skills when they immigrated. Vineyards have prospered and produce some fine wines, using both imported and native grapes. A restored jail in Paris houses a small museum that depicts more of the region's history.

The first stop in Paris should be **The Grapevine Restaurant,** owned by Kenneth and Linda Vines, a brother-and-sister team cooking great food there on Highway 22. Smoked meats, fresh-baked bread and cinnamon rolls, and sinfully delicious desserts join healthy fresh vegetables. Handwritten menus announce the daily specials. Linda seems to know everyone in town and can direct you to the wineries and other interesting places to visit. The restaurant is open from 9:00 A.M. to 9:00 P.M. Tuesday through Thursday, from 9:00 A.M. to 10:00 P.M. Friday and Saturday, and from 11:00 A.M. to 3:00 P.M. Sunday, with Sunday brunch and a luncheon special. The Grapevine is at 105 East Walnut; call (501) 963–2413.

Three clothing shops and a shoe store make it easy to buy Paris fashions in the shopping area downtown on the square. You can also send postcards from Paris to impress your friends. Tell them you are about to enter wine country—they'll be green with envy.

Then seek forgiveness for the little white lie at the graceful **Subiaco Abbey** in the tiny town of Subiaco, 3 miles east of Paris on Highway 22. The stone and red-tile-roof abbey is a Benedictine academy built in 1878 and is the only monastery in the state. It was built, by the monks, of locally quarried sandstone. Marble and stained glass imported from Europe accent the fine rockwork. The abbey rises dramatically from the farmlands surrounding it, and the seventy monks welcome visitors to tour the church and courtyard and see the museum of local history. The Coury House at the abbey offers guests a retreat wherein you can take time to meditate and relax without the distraction of even a telephone. Rooms are $30.00 and up with private baths; meals in the guest dining hall are available for $4.00. The academy is a boys' prep school for grades nine through twelve. According to Brother Mel, a monk at the academy, there are also organized retreats: marriage encounters and prayer retreats with monks or different denominational groups who use the facility throughout the year. The monks' mass is at 6:30 A.M. every morning and open to the public; Sunday mass is at 10:45 A.M. Call Jean Rockenhaus, the abbey secretary, at (501) 934–4411 for a schedule of retreats or for room reservations.

Scenic Highway 22 runs along the river connecting Paris and Dardanelle and is a beautiful side trip to get you off the freeway and into the countryside. It cuts across some of the coves of Lake Dardanelle and through the Ouachita National Forest.

Dardanelle is a historic old river town on the banks of the Arkansas River and Lake Dardanelle at the crossroads of Scenic

Highways 7 and 22. Steamboat passengers landed at Dardanelle a century ago. The road climbing Mount Nebo's steep slopes were narrow, with hairpin turns, but the scenery and cool breezes made the trip worth the effort. Arkansas summers can be hot, and this was a great escape. It still is. The town sits at the hub of three state parks.

Mount Nebo State Park, on Highway 155 South, up gorgeous Mount Nebo, is a fine spot to get the feel of the Arkansas wilderness. This is the state's highest state park, with panoramic views of the valley. Ten rustic cabins dating from the Civilian Conservation Corps era, as well as four modern A-frames, are scattered around the top of the mountain above the Arkansas River Valley. Many of the cabins are very secluded and quiet, while others are very, *very* secluded and quiet. The park is lovely, containing a large lake with the pine forest coming right down to the shoreline. The beautiful lake is spotted with islands and surrounded by softly wooded land. The park commands a terrific view from atop a plateau 1,800 feet above the river. Cabins rent for $40 to $55. Call (501) 229–3655.

Lake Dardanelle State Park on Highway 326 allows campers to stake out shoreline sites at the campgrounds. Skiers and sailboats crisscross the water, while fishermen anchor in coves, casting for bream, crappie, and bass. Recordmaking monster catfish weighing in excess of forty pounds are caught here under the dam. The oldest state fishing record was set in 1964, when someone caught a 215-pound alligator gar on the Arkansas River near Dardanelle (he was using a minnow). The river here has sandy beaches and river access for boats on Highway 22 West.

Beyond the city of Dardanelle lies flat-topped Petit Jean Mountain near Morrilton. Petit Jean State Park, on top of the mountain, has eight rustic cabins and five modern duplexes. These are not as secluded as the ones at Mount Nebo. In fact a couple of them are near the highway, but there's little traffic there at night. They rent for $50. Mather Lodge, inside the park, has twenty-four rooms and a restaurant. The lodge is poised on the rim of Cedar Creek Canyon, and hiking paths weave more than 24 miles throughout the park.

Trails lead to the picture-perfect, 90-foot-high **Cedar Falls** within Cedar Creek Canyon; to delicate sandstone monoliths; and to Rock House Cave, containing ancient pictographs etched into stone by early inhabitants of the area. The falls are spectacular and

Cedar Falls

worth the trip to see. The best time to photograph them is in late afternoon when the sun shines directly onto the spectacular falls and reflects sunlight in crystal sparkles. (During the morning hours the mighty falls are shaded and dark.) The falls are created by rainwater caught in the saucer-shaped mountaintop.

The park gets its name from the legend of Adrienne DuMont, a French girl who disguised herself as a boy (calling herself Jean) and accompanied her sailor sweetheart to America. She died before the return trip and was buried on the mountain. There is an unmarked grave on the mountain, and the legend begins there.

The **Museum of Automobiles,** also at Petit Jean Mountain, displays privately owned antique and classic automobiles from collectors throughout the country and abroad. The museum was founded by Governor Winthrop Rockefeller and features some of his personal cars. The place is in a constant state of change, so you can visit it again and again if you are an auto buff. There are memories here in chrome and leather, as well as cars you've only heard about. The facility is open year-round from 10:00 A.M. to 5:00 P.M. and has a gift shop on the premises. Call (501) 727–5427.

Tanyard Springs, on Highway 154 on the west edge of Petit Jean Mountain, calls itself "The Un-Resort" and lives up to that billing with thirteen rustic-looking but handcrafted cottages, each different and each designed to fit the setting. None of the natural beauty of the area has been changed; the cottages are tucked into the woods near a stream or a pond. Big porches with swings and rocking chairs allow the sounds of the woods to penetrate even the most stressed-out soul. Each cottage is perfectly reproduced in incredible detail, with wood-carvings, handcrafted antique furnishings, and accessories to insure historical accuracy. Each is also decorated around a theme. The most unusual, Stagecoach Cottage, actually has a full-size Butterfield stagecoach as a bed in the loft (the kids will love it). But these are more than just rustic cabins (that's why they're carefully referred to as "cottages," not cabins), as the price will tell you right away—from $125 during the week to $150 on weekends, with a two-night minimum. Inside lies an interior as comfortable as any fine city hotel's, with cleverly hidden appliances and large, comfortable beds.

Adrienne's Restaurant, inside the compound, serves fine cuisine from 5:30 to 9:00 P.M. nightly and is so small and intimate that, as with the cottages, you definitely need a reservation well in advance. Because the township is dry this is a private club, but membership is only $5.00 and the wine list is excellent. So is the food, with entrees like Veal Adrienne in a muscadine and Dijon cream sauce, or trout almandine with amaretto sauce. The resort and restaurant are not a mom-and-pop operation, obviously; they are owned by Winthrop Paul Rockefeller, son of the late governor, and the cottages are all carefully tucked behind a security gate. The place has its own landing strip for those coming in by private plane. Sometimes getting off the beaten path costs a little more—in this case it's worth it. Call (800) 533–1450 or 727–5200 for reservations.

South of Petit Jean Mountain on Highway 9 and about 40 miles west of Little Rock off Highway 10, the unique walking trail among the wildflowers at the **Heifer Project International Learning and Livestock Center** gives you a chance

71

to learn how sunlight can be harnessed, bricks made of earth, and weeds thatched for roofing; how livestock can be raised in poor areas of the world; and how poor soil can be made to produce food. A longer hike along the wooded hillside will show sites where fish are raised in cages and horses pull plows. The Guatemala Hillside, a farmhouse on two and a half steep, eroded acres, has blossomed into a farm with five species of livestock, ten tree crops, and more than fifteen annual crops and vegetables. Water harvesting and biogas fuel are a few of the innovative processes. The 1,225-acre ranch includes Brangus cattle and Katahdin hair sheep. There are hands-on teaching units of swine to be slopped, goats to be milked, and poultry, rabbits, and bees to be tended. Informal visits can be made anytime, and a guided tour of the small-farm project can be arranged. A working visit, internship, or volunteer experience can also be arranged by calling the trail coordinator at (501) 889–5124. Signs will lead you to the center from Highway 10.

North Bank Wine Country

Cross to the north side of the Arkansas River at Morrilton and head back west on Highway 64, which parallels I–40. You will be following the same route the Butterfield Overland Stage followed. There's an old stagecoach at Ninth and College streets in Pottsville, one of many that used to be headed for **Potts Tavern,** now a museum downtown. The beautifully restored, antebellum house was a stagecoach stop and tavern on the Butterfield Overland Stage route. But there's more: It is also one of the only two *hat* museums in the country, if sombreros are your fetish. Five log cabins have been moved onto the property—one is the caretaker's home. Hours are from 1:00 to 5:00 P.M. Tuesday through Saturday.

Right across the street the Pottsville Grocery Store, at Second and Ash, is more an old-fashioned general store, with groceries, hardware, plumbing supplies, and gifts in this tiny town. Aliene Morton owns it, and she says she "kinda takes care of people when no one's at the museum across the street." You can pick up all the supplies you need at Aliene's and garner any information about the area from her. You can usually find her and a few other folks watching the television in the front of the store. Hours are from 7:00 A.M. to 6:00 P.M. (sometimes later) seven days a week; call (501) 968–6703.

Russellville, on Highway 64, is small-town friendly, maybe because it's a college town, home of Arkansas Tech University. **River Valley Arts Center,** at B and Knoxville streets in a natural stone building built by the Civilian Conservation Corps in the 1930s, is a former swimming pool/bathhouse that is now a gallery and more. There are two galleries, actually: the Artists' Gallery, which displays the work of ten or twelve local artists every month, and the Main Gallery, which features one-person shows of well-known artists, such as Ansel Adams or Leonard Baskin, a Works Progress Administration artist of the 1930s whose work changed art in America. The gallery displays work from every medium—two- and three-dimensional art, weaving, sculpting, and photography. But there is more: Truly a center for the arts in the area, it has a community theater, a band, and a chamber chorus. There are educational arts programs, as well as the only pottery program in the state that is staffed year-round, for both children and adults. Associations like the River Valley Writers' Club, a songwriters' group, and an artists' support group meet here. The center is open from Tuesday through Friday from 10:00 A.M. to 6:00 P.M.; call (501) 968–2452.

Russellville is the place to find Ozark handicrafts, too. **Ozark Heritage Craft Village,** just off I–40 on Highway 7, carries artisans' handiwork from across the state. Everything is handmade—quilts, dolls, wooden toys, pottery, and baskets, to name just a few. The old-time atmosphere and folks in period dress who know the historical features of the area, as well as demonstrations from time to time, make it a good place to stop. Hours vary with the season but are roughly from 8:30 A.M. to 5:00 P.M.; call (501) 967–3232.

Ready for a sandwich? **Stoby's** is a one-of-a-kind place—a 1941 Rock Island dining car parked at a red brick and stucco depot, a replica of the real thing across the way. It's open for breakfast, lunch, and dinner with a menu that is both ordinary and extraordinary. Take the Stoby's sandwich, for example. The number of meats, cheeses, breads, and toppings totals 3,000 possible combinations, according to the computer. There're a full breakfast menu and homemade pies and cakes, since Stoby's opens at 6:00 A.M. and stays open until 10:00 P.M. every day except Sunday. Casual is the keyword here, according to manager Richard Bailey. He calls the place an "unusual combination of familiar things." It's just the right combination of quick food and full service, with prices in the very comfortable zone. You'll find Stoby's 2 miles south of I–40 on Highway 7, at 405 West D Street; call (501) 968–3816.

Jimmy Lile's Handmade Knives is 2 miles south of Russellville on Highway 7 South. Before his recent death Jimmy Lile was considered one of the top five custom knifemakers in the world; Lile was the designer and maker of the knives used in the *Rambo* movies, and this shop and showroom are filled with examples of his craft. Four presidents, the king of Sweden, and many people in the entertainment industry own his knives. Lile's knives are well recognized worldwide and are still being handcrafted by skilled workers trained by Lile. Mrs. Lile runs the business of making all manner of knives—folders, hunting knives of all kinds with 4- to 6-inch blades, and both drop-point and upswept blades. She personally oversees the business. According to the people in the shop, she considers herself "inspector number twelve—it's not finished till she says so." Hours are from 9:00 A.M. to 4:30 P.M. Monday through Friday. Lile's is located at 721 South Arkansas Avenue; call (501) 968–2011.

Big Piney Creek, near Russellville, is a small stream flowing from the wilderness of the Ozark National Forest to the Arkansas River. Canoes and white-water rafts float on gentle tributaries like Big Piney and the Illinois Bayou. You can take a trip down Big Piney winding along spectacular granite bluffs from Fallsville through the mountains and into Lake Dardanelle. Short afternoon floats or several-day trips can also be arranged. Although the Big Piney's 67-mile route has Class II and III rapids—the first, Split Decision, to the grand finale, Haystacker Rapid—it can be enjoyed by both the beginner and the experienced white-water paddler (areas containing Class III rapids need white-water experience). You can call the Big Piney Creek outpost at Moore Outdoors (501–331–3606), 10 miles north of Dover on Highway 164 West. Kerry and Debbie Moore have canoes, wetsuits, helmets, throwlines, dry bags, and other white-water accessories (for experienced people), as well as camping equipment and kayak lessons; the Moores will also shuttle hikers to the Ozark Highland Trail by the Ozone or Richmond campground. The creek is at its finest from March through May and, in wet years, sometimes as late as Thanksgiving. Moore Outdoors is open from 8:30 A.M. to 6:00 P.M. seven days a week in season.

North of Clarksville on Highway 21, the little town of Ozone is home to some very strange creatures. Exotic animals fill **Shadow Lake Ranch.** A couple of years ago, Ethel and Laurence Nauman and their son Michael moved from Wyoming to Ozone. They brought their minihorses (16 to 34 inches tall) and miniature donkeys with them. It wasn't long before they had added a couple of expensive llamas (llamas get lonely and don't like to be single), some longhorn cattle, and a couple of fainting goats, those strange little creatures that swoon when frightened. The stock supply grew. Potbellied pigs, white-tailed deer, and Sika deer—the kind that retain their spots and stay fawnlike—joined the ranch. Now the Naumans invite people to stop by the ranch and feed and touch the little creatures.

Ethel's love of all creatures great and small is obvious when visitors see the "Odd Couple," a white-tailed deer and a potbellied pig that are inseparable. It seems that the fawn was rescued from dogs and very frightened, so Ethel put the runt of the potbellied pig litter, who was not getting her share of motherly love either, in with the fawn. The fawn began to lick the pig, and soon the pig was sleeping on the fawn's neck at night. Both were bottle-fed and the bonding was immediate. Ethel tells of trying to register her 14-inch-tall fainting goats, requiring a photograph of each of them with four legs in the air. She says she just couldn't do it—"I couldn't build their trust, then yell `boo' and cause them to stiffen and drop over." Consequently most of her herd is not registered.

Guarding the 240-acre ranch and 10-acre lake is Daisy, a Great Pyrenees who is not miniature at all. This well-over-a-hundred-pound dog is the size of a St. Bernard and trained to circle the herd at night and guard the area. Her bark, almost a yodel when she's really excited, is warning enough for most people. The ranch is 1 mile east of Ozone on Porter Road, but the Naumans suggest calling ahead (501–292–3648) for specific directions.

The 187-mile Ozark Highland Trail passes nearby, and a campground is about 5 miles from the ranch. Ethel can give you directions for the beautiful drive, although on a gravel road, from Shadow Lake to the **Bunkhouse Mulberry Ranch** in Oark, which is about 20 miles north of Clarksville on Highway 103 North. This secluded, 120-acre cattle ranch in the Boston Mountains, surrounded by national forest, with the Mulberry River meandering through for white-water canoeing, belongs to Doug and Susan Pfeifler, who have a cabin on the ranch with two bed-

The "Odd Couple" at Shadow Lake Ranch

rooms, a bathroom, a greatroom, and a fireplace. The kitchen is supplied with home-baked bread, as well as eggs and bacon, for those who want to cook up a regular country breakfast. The kitchen is also stocked with soft drinks, a full cookie jar, and a fruit bowl, and first-night late arrivals are offered a crockpot of chili or stew. The cabin appeals to honeymooners, anniversary couples, or groups of young people. A private swimming hole on the river, with picnic area and barbecue and an abundance of smallmouth and largemouth bass and catfish to cook right there, is nearby. The Pfeiflers live in another house on the property. Call (501) 292–3725 for reservations and directions. The cost of the cabin is $65 for two, plus $15 for each additional adult and $10 for each child over five years old.

The drive to the cabin is through the beautiful valley, past farm country where cattle graze beside the roadway. There's even an old-fashioned country general store down the way a bit for odds and ends you might need. The twisting road curves up the Boston Mountains and tops out near Batson, then starts downhill again to the valley. It's about a forty-minute drive.

The Ozark Highland Trail, running through the most remote and scenic wilderness in the Ozarks, has several access points nearby, and Doug or Susan will be happy to drop you there. It is a well-marked trail, and you can choose easy and short sections or longer overnight hikes that could take several days.

The center of wine country on the north bank of the Arkansas River lies along Highway 64. Altus (which means "altitude") is the highest point between Little Rock and Fort Smith. Swiss and German settlers arrived during the 1880s and blanketed the valley with grapevines. Wineries dot the valley today and continue the tradition. Although not as well known, the 12,000-acre Altus region is a registered wine-producing region like Napa and Sonoma. There are tours and tastings year-round, together with festivals celebrating the harvest and barefoot grape-stomping contests among the families who own the wineries.

Post Familie Winery, 1 block north of Highway 64 on Highway 186, was founded in 1880. Winemaking tours take visitors through the process from grape to cork. The prolific Post family has twelve children, all grown now and, for the most part, all in the wine business. A variety of grapes, both those native to the state and those harder to grow here, are produced in the vineyards. The French cabernet grape is hand-picked and lovingly cared for; it is at risk this far east, as a hard winter could destroy the root stock. But so far it is growing well, producing a wine that will surprise even connoisseurs. The Cynthiana grape, with its bright color and distinctive flavor, is, on the other hand, native to the valley.

The winery has an interesting gift shop and carries local crafts, as well as clever handmade gift items like wooden airplanes and trucks designed to be used as wine bottle holders. Quilts, grape leaves brushed with gold and made into earrings and pendants, and even smoked trout make the gift shop and tasting room worth a stop.

Continuing up the mountain on Highway 186 will bring you to **St. Mary's Mountain Bed and Breakfast,** at 501 St. Mary's Mountain Road, where Mayor Joy Wilcox and her daughter Heidi have a house with three guest rooms tucked back off the road. The bedrooms on the second floor are separated by a 500-square-foot hallway where complimentary local wine is kept cold and breakfast blueberry coffeecake, cinnamon rolls, and other treats are kept warm. A coffee and tea pot is in each room. The common area has a refrigerator and a microwave, along with books and cable television. Joy even has a guitar and marimba if you feel like making your own music. Locally made crafts are displayed here, too, and are for sale. Rooms cost $39. Call (501) 468–4141 for reservations.

Highway 186 winds up the mountain to **Wiederkehr Village,** a Swiss Alpine–style village, home of the Wiederkehr Winery. The Weinkeller Restaurant is in the winery's original wine cellar, dug by Johann Andreas Wiederkehr in 1880 and listed on the National Register of Historic Places. A romantic little candlelit spot, it offers German food Tyrolean-style—the grandfather was from German-speaking Switzerland—such as schnitzel and German fried potatoes and wines carefully aged in oak. Hours Monday through Saturday are from 11:00 A.M. to 3:00 P.M. for lunch and from 5:00 to 10:00 P.M. for dinner; Sunday hours are from noon to 9:00 P.M. Call (501) 468–3551 for restaurant reservations.

Tours of the winery itself leave every hour and half-hour from 9:00 A.M. to 4:30 P.M. Monday through Saturday. The huge winery covers 350 acres and produces 100,000 cases of wine a year. The annual wine festival, held the last Saturday in September, is worth a trip to join, with polka bands and a grape-stomping contest among the winery families of the valley. Call Linda Wiederkehr at (501) 468–2611 for more information.

At the crest of the hill is St. Mary's Catholic Church, built by the Germans who fled the Franco-Prussian war. The church is built of local sandstone and trimmed with gold leaf. It has a wonderful old pipe organ. Built in 1901, the church is on the National Register of Historic Places. It's open from 8:00 A.M. till 6:00 P.M. so that visitors can see the famous murals inside, done with local people as models (many folks here recognize great-uncles, -aunts, and grandparents).

The trip up to Wiederkehr isn't the last of the wineries, though. **Mount Bethel Winery** is 0.25 mile east of Altus on Highway 64. Eugene and Peggy Post and their eight grown children are current owners. It was the original Post Winery but is now an entirely separate winery. The grown children come back to help at harvest time, when 15,000 gallons of wine are made here. Mostly sweet wines and fruit wines like blackberry and wild plum, these screw-cap wines make no pretensions to greatness. But the Golden Muscat Port is similar to the Lagrima ports of Portugal, a very light and fruity wine, fortified with brandy to keep in a decanter for slow sipping. Call (501) 468–2444 for information.

If you have time for a side trip, turn north on Highway 282 (it parallels Highway 71) near Van Buren and drive to Mountainburg. The route is steep and winding, with sharp turns, and provides glimpses of genuine log cabins—the kind with mud between the logs—hidden in the trees. The housing may not be modern, but folks living in these cabins have the kind of view out the back window that people in other parts of the country pay millions to have. There is a spectacular view of Lake Fort Smith, Lake Shepherd Springs, and the river that makes them.

The White Mountain Wildlife Management Area is nearby, and 8 miles north of Mountainburg you will find Artist Point, on scenic Saddle Canyon of Highway 71, with an overlook that offers a view of the Boston Mountains that is a photographer's dream. The tiny gift shop there (501–369–2226) has a bit of everything, including homemade jams as well as a historical Indian museum.

Highway 71 near Mountainburg (Highways 282 and 71 come together there) is the first Ozark Mountain Smokehouse to open in the state. This is where Frank Sharp began the enterprise that has expanded into a mail-order business and a string of rustic-appearing restaurants and shops that hide a very modern operation inside. Smoked turkey is the specialty. Frank introduced the sandwich buffet, where customers make their own sandwiches and pay by the ounce. The smokehouse makes bread, pastries, desserts, and even fruit preserves. The phone number is easy to remember: 800–HAM–SHOP.

The **Ozark Highlands Trail** begins in Lake Fort Smith State Park, which is deeply nestled in a wooded valley of the Boston Mountains. This trail offers hiking and backpacking through the Ozark National Forest, a 187-mile adventure as challenging as one anywhere else in the country. The scenery along the trail is outstanding, with hundreds of streams and more than 200 waterfalls and pools. Rambling through remote and rugged land, the trail is dotted by access points with parking and passes through eight campgrounds. There are several ways to go: A short day hike up White Rock Mountain will give you a pretty sunset, or begin at Shores Lake and take the 6-mile spur trail up to White Rock and spend the night. Hare Mountain lets you explore the remains of an 1800s homesite via a 6-mile hike from Highway 23 or a 2-mile walk from Hare Mountain Trailhead. One of the most beautiful spots, however, is the Marinoni Scenic Area, where the trail hugs a steep hillside and overlooks a creek. The Hurricane Creek Wilderness Area has deep green pools connected by white water and surrounded by towering bluffs. Swimming in the pools; lying on the large, smooth rocks; playing in waterfalls; going hunting, fishing, and camping—all are there. The *Ozark Highlands Trail Guide*—a 104-page handbook with maps, elevations, and mileage logs; information on scenic spots and campgrounds; weather guide; and an animal and insect guide—is available at the Visitors' Center. The center even has a Rent-a-Backpack program, but the Evans Point Loop, a 7-mile trail circling the lake, is there for those who don't want to go overnight on the trail. The park has six cabins near a large group lodge. From I–40 take exit 13 at Alma and go 12 miles north on Highway 71 to just north of Mountainburg. For cabin reservations call (501) 369–2469; prices are $35 to $40.

Fort Smith and Van Buren, founded in 1818, are next-door neighbors. But there is so much to see in Van Buren's beautifully preserved Main Street Historic District that you can just plan to spend a day there. The town was called Steamboat Landing or Phillips Landing and was a stop on the Butterfield Stage Line from St. Louis to California. The name Van Buren was to honor Martin Van Buren, but, interestingly enough, the naming occurred before he was president—he was just a friend of Phillips then. Main Street in Van Buren is a restored delight, bustling with shops and restaurants and some of the best antiques shopping around. It still retains its original nineteenth-century charm and has been used as the location for filming such movies as *The Blue and the Gray, Biloxi Blues,* and *Main Street Van Buren.* Stay on Main Street and sample what Van Buren has to offer.

The Cottage Cafe, at 810 Main, has been a favorite hangout for a long time. It features biscuits and gravy, as well as homemade pies like chocolate peanut butter, pecan, and egg custard. The cozy atmosphere and friendly, down-home feeling make it the logical place to get the feel of the town. People there tend to be local folks and can give you directions to and information about the other places along Main Street. The cafe is right across the street from the Old Frisco Depot, too; call (501) 474–9895.

A vintage train excursion on the **Ozark Scenic Railway** takes visitors on day trips from the Old Frisco Depot (1901), at 813 Main, to the beauty of the Ozark Mountains. The 18-mile round-trip to Rudy takes one hour ($12.00), and the 70-mile round-trip to Winslow takes three hours ($24.50). You will pass over three high trestles and then go through a mountain tunnel surrounded by the lush Ozarks. Reservations can be made by calling (501) 474–2761.

The King Opera House in the historic district is home to the King Opera House Players and, they say, the ghost of a traveling actor who was shot and killed by the father of a young lady about to run away with him in the 1880s.

There's another ghost in town, too. Rumor has it that an "unseen presence" inhabits the second floor of the **Old Van Buren Inn Bed and Breakfast and Restaurant** owned by Jackie Henningsen, a native of California who came here and decided to stay when she saw the Old Crawford Bank Building at 633 Main Street in the historic district. Jackie found the ghost "friendly, so far," and decided to share the apparition with others. So she opened a California-style eatery and made the second story into a bed-and-breakfast. She's done quite a job on the old bank building, renovating it herself with hours of help from family and friends.

The restaurant is open and sunny, and the food is truly as "California" as the middle of the country can get. Meals are light and flavorful. Bean sprouts and avocados appear; small salads are crisp and delicate; there's quiche, of course; and the homemade desserts—well, as they say on the West Coast, the apple dumpling is "to die for." The restaurant is open from 9:00 A.M. to 5:00 P.M. Monday through Saturday and from noon to 4:00 P.M. Sunday.

There are three rooms available upstairs in the B & B, and each is filled with a soft bed, a rocking chair, and good books. The Victorian furnishings were hand-selected from antiques shops in the South. There're a half-bath in the hall and a large sunlight- and plant-filled bathroom with a double tub. Call (501) 474–4202 for reservations. Rooms are priced from $47 to $75.

CRAWFORD COUNTY BANK

Cathy Johnson

Old Van Buren Inn Bed and Breakfast and Restaurant

Artist Ramonia Mitchell's shop, Visual Enterprise, at 610 Main Street, is a quiet little gallery featuring Steve Payne's oils, along with much pottery, wood, and other artistic pieces. It's open from 10:30 A.M. to 4:00 P.M. Tuesday through Saturday. Call (501) 474-3358.

The Antique Warehouse Mall, at 402 Main Street, is the kind of place you can wander around in for hours. Jerry Sounders, manager, says that most of the things in the front of the shop are imported from England, Ireland, and Scotland. The two huge back rooms are filled by the wares of twenty dealers; there are dozens of stained glass windows back there, too. The operation is one of the largest importers in the Ozarks and has a complete restoration service. Call (501) 474-4808.

After checking out all the shops on Main Street and the rest of the historic district, walk down toward the river, across the tracks, to the wall that protects the town from the Arkansas River. There, overlooking the river, is a park where you can relax and enjoy the soothing sounds of the river. But while you are contemplating the river, turn around and look at the back side of the wall and you will see a mural depicting the history of Van Buren, painted by local high school students.

Off the Beaten Path in Southwest Arkansas

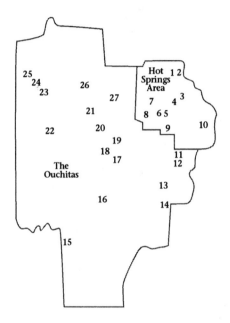

1. Herbs Plus
2. Polly's Everlastings
3. Fox Pass Pottery
4. Hot Springs
5. Stillmeadow Farm
6. Mountain Brook Stables
7. Mid-America Museum
8. Second Chance Farm
9. The Owl Prowl
10. Feathered Nest Wildlife Farm
11. Something Special
12. Glover's Candy Kitchen
13. International Order of Hoo-Hoos Museum
14. White Oak Lake State Park
15. Hog Heaven
16. Old Washington Historic State Park
17. Crater of Diamonds State Park
18. Ka-Do-Ha Indian Village
19. Bear Creek Cycle Trail
20. Country School Inn
21. Little Missouri Falls
22. "Beauty and the Beast"
23. Ansata Arabian Stud Farm
24. Talimena Drive
25. Queen Wilhelmina Lodge
26. Lum and Abner Museum
27. Wegner Quartz Crystal Mines

Southwest Arkansas

Western Arkansas's mountains, caves, and rolling hills provide the perfect terrain for those who enjoy rappelling, spelunking, serious hiking, biking, or just general messing around outdoors. The upper Ouachita River is a boulder-strewn stream with plenty of riffles and gravel bars. As the river turns south, it gets slower and deeper and forms three lakes: Ouachita, Hamilton, and Catherine.

The Diamond Lakes region covers five counties and contains five surprisingly uncrowded lakes, as well as the Caddo, Ouachita, and Saline rivers. Water babies will revel in the lakes, streams, and rivers loaded with bass and catfish and perfect for fishing, boating, water-skiing, canoeing, rafting, or just wading.

The Cossatot River crashes through here. It is called "Beauty and the Beast" because of its Class V rapids of crystal-clear white water. Definitely not for beginners.

Don't be tempted to take the easy way through the southwest corner of the state on I–30—try some backroads. This dense piney woodland area is alive with natural attractions and some of the state's most exciting history. The old Southwest Trail passed through here, as did men as famous as Colonel James Bowie, Stephen F. Austin, Davy Crockett, and Sam Houston on their way to Texas.

Hot Springs Area

Highway 7 squiggles through the mountains. Distances are deceiving on the map, so allow plenty of time if you want to get in before dark. Come into the Ouachita Mountains on Scenic Highway 7 and slow down about 3 miles north of Jessieville to watch for the signs leading to **Herbs Plus,** Kathy Seitz's hundred-acre herb farm; the barn-shaped building is not visible from the highway, so watch for signs leading to it or you might miss it. Sachets, herbal vinegar, and plants as well as fresh-cut herbs are for sale. This is not a medicinal herb shop; the sweet-smelling spices and herbs are meant for cooking. Herbs Plus also offers cooking classes lasting from about 10:00 A.M. to 2:00 P.M. These classes cost $15 and include enjoying the meal that is cooked. Classes are designed for about ten people and are especially popular now with the trend toward cooking with less salt and fat. Call (501) 984–5740 for a schedule of classes.

Upstairs you'll find **Polly's Everlastings,** where Polly Felker creates dried floral bouquets, wreaths, "tussie mussie" (a Victorian nosegay), and all-natural potpourri (no wood chips). These delicate florals surprisingly retain the true colors of the flowers from which they are made. Drying flowers hang in bunches from the ceiling (and can be purchased to create your own designs), and wreaths and bouquets cover the walls. Most of the flowers are symbolic—Victorian women kept a dictionary of meanings—and so Polly attaches a note explaining them for gifts, the meanings ranging from congratulations to sympathy. She uses herbs, flowers, and wild grasses to form the arrangements, and many are done by special order. Polly says these delicate florals can be packed for traveling. The shop also has antiques, collectible dolls, quilts, and other items brought in by Nancy Knotek, who travels about collecting them. The shop is open Tuesday through Friday from 10:00 A.M. to 5:00 P.M. and Saturday from 9:00 A.M. to 3:00 P.M.; it is closed from just before Christmas until February 1.

Fox Pass Pottery, off Highway 7 on Fox Pass Cutoff, is also the home of Jim and Barbara Larkin. They have lived in the stone house attached to the studio and surrounded by national forest for eighteen years. The Larkins use local quartz for glazing and silica sand from the White River in their creations. Barbara is the creator of "Bud and Babe," a quirky twosome who show up frequently in her work in various guises. (Bud carries a cigar in his teeth and will show up on a "Bud vase" as well as in sculptures; Babe looks just as the name implies.) Jim creates more functional items. His colanders, mugs, and vases are fired in the kilns he built himself: The "bisque kiln" is the first step—it goes to 1,800 degrees, then cools. Then the "car kiln" reaches 2,400 degrees for the glaze; this kiln takes sixteen hours and two days to cool. To visit the studio turn onto the gravel road across from the red mill and go 0.5 mile down Fox Pass Cutoff. Hours are Monday through Saturday from 9:00 A.M. to 5:00 P.M.; call (501) 623–9906.

That red mill is the Old Mill Gift Shop across Highway 7 from the Fox Pass turnoff. It's full of items made by more than a hundred Arkansas craftspeople. Here you'll find dolls of every type—hickory, corncob, apple-head, and hand-carved wooden dolls as well as rag dolls. The waterwheel operates in the old mill stream outside the door. Call (501) 623–4710 for information.

As it enters **Hot Springs,** Highway 7 is lined with big old homes set back on deep lots high on hills. The highway becomes Central Avenue and Bathhouse Row when it gets into town. Here's a city where you can have your palm read, enjoy a bath and massage, get married, or go to the races at Oaklawn—or all of the above. And there are plenty of good restaurants for a city so small.

Hot Springs was the hot spot in its day, no question. During Prohibition the Valley of the Vapors had bathtub gin, clanging electric trolley cars, speakeasies, and painted women. It was an odd combination of shady entertainment along Central Avenue: One side was shady as in illegal; the other side, a shady national park managed by federal rangers.

People have been bathing at the spa since Hernando de Soto did in 1541. But he was just doing what the Native Americans had always done. According to legend the Indians soaked in steaming pools when they talked peace with warring tribes. Through the years traders, trappers, politicians, and gangsters have soaked in these waters. By the 1900s Bathhouse Row's most elegant establishment was the Spanish Renaissance Revival–style Fordyce Bathhouse, where water bubbled up from deep in the earth's center, reaching the surface at 143 degrees, whereupon it was cooled for bathing. Fordyce Bathhouse visitors' center was restored by the National Park Service at a cost of $5 million; the elegant bathing facility is now open to the public—although you can't have a bath there today.

The 4,800-acre Hot Springs National Park visitors' center in the restored bathhouse has the decadent legacy of that bygone day. The only gambling done now takes place at Oaklawn Park during the spring thoroughbred racing season, although dinner in the circa 1875 Arlington Hotel's Venetian Room might help you replay some of that feeling under glimmering chandeliers, with jazz drifting in from the lobby bar.

This is the very place where Al Capone headquartered his gang during Prohibition days. Veined Italian marble, wrought iron, and hardwood railings are everywhere, along with classical sculptures and ornate ceramics. The third floor sunroom is the true showstopper, with its stained glass, vaulted ceiling, grand piano, and wicker furniture. And the promenade behind Bathhouse Row is a nice place to stroll. The visitors' center is open from 8:00 A.M. until 5:00 P.M. daily (until 6:00 P.M. in summer). Call (501) 623–1433.

People came from miles around for the mineral water baths (health seekers, they claimed to be), so to fill the time between baths, gambling houses were run by the underworld of Chicago, New York, and Miami. The 1886 Majestic Hotel, 1 block away, is where "Bugs" Moran, Capone's rival, hung out. Today you can still "take the waters" in the warm steamy bathhouse there. If you are lucky, you will meet Jim Lemons, who has been a bath attendant there for almost sixty years, or Kathleen Crowe, across the hall in the beauty parlor, where she has been giving facials for almost forty-five years. The two of them delight customers with stories of the gangsters of the era while one is soaked, massaged, and pampered.

The visitors' center downtown at 600 Central is a good place to start touring. Pearl Ridgeway is there just about every day and plans to be so unless "they kick me out or close the place." She can help you find anything you want. There are many antiques shops on Central Avenue if you want to browse. You can call Pearl at (501) 321–9763 for more information about the city. The center is open from 9:30 A.M. to 5:00 P.M. Monday through Saturday ; on Sundays the center is open from 1:00 to 5:00 P.M.

Hot Springs is still a resort town, so there is more entertainment here than in other cities this size. Good live-music places in town range from the soft strains of Marian Moss in the Terrace Room of the Majestic Hotel to the Cajun-spiced scene at Shakey Jake's on Central Avenue for some serious partying. And as for eating, well, you've come to the right place.

Café New Orleans, at 210 Central, is a small café across the street from the Arlington Hotel and reminiscent of the Café du Monde in New Orleans's Vieux Carré. The high ceilings, concrete floors, small tables along mirrored walls, and, of course, a coffee bar give this old 1885 saloon the feel of Crescent City. Trays of *beignets,* coated with powdered sugar and served hot, and good café au lait await you.

Allan Kaylo and Sig Grossman have owned the place for three years. It started as a coffeehouse, but Allan missed the food back in the Big Easy (New Orleans). He now serves the best of the Cajun food in the cafe and on the patio out back Sunday through Thursday from 7:00 A.M. to 9:00 P.M. and Friday and Saturday to 10:00 P.M. Call (501) 624–3200.

89

Mollie's, at 538 West Grand, may be the only place in Arkansas to get tasty, kosher-style cooking. The white brick house looks deceptively small, but the back of the house overlooks the garden area, where patio dining is offered in good weather. There is more than just healing chicken soup, though. Owner Betty Forshberg (whose mother-in-law was the original Mollie) also serves a fine brisket of beef, potato pancakes, cheese blintzes, and, of course, chopped liver. Mollie's is open from 11:00 A.M. to 9:30 P.M. every day but Sunday. Call (501) 623–6582.

A favorite place with the cognoscenti is McClard's, at 505 Albert Pike. This is an unassuming place with bright lights and, according to locals, the best barbecue in the state. The 1950s diner is always crowded, and with good reason: Not only is the barbecue great, but the tamale spread is fiery hot and, with a cold beer, hard to beat. Call (501) 624–9586.

But "man does not live by bread alone." Hot Springs has recently become a fine arts center for the state. A Gallery Walk, held the first Thursday of each month, is gallery open-house night to meet with artists whose works are being shown. About twenty fine arts galleries and arts-related businesses participate in the walk; refreshments are served, too. The Hot Springs Fine Arts Center, situated in an 1891 building at 514 Central Avenue, is the heart of the city's art renaissance. Call Marla Crider for more information about the walk: (501) 321–2835.

At 700 Central, Maxine's International Coffee House caters to the artistic set. The art gallery in the restaurant changes exhibits each month, and on the Thursday night of Gallery Walk this is the only place to sit down and have an Amaretto coffee (or sandwich, or beer or wine) while enjoying a gallery exhibit. Thursday night is also open forum night—the piano and mike are open to customers. If you want to read poetry or play a little jazz piano, this is the spot for you.

Perhaps the place is not as lively as it used to be back when the original Maxine had a bordello upstairs, but current owners Robert and Ormell Sabo do enjoy playing chess and checkers with customers. Their daughter Brendee Babin is the manager, and she loves to entertain customers with magic tricks. In fact her favorite is the "rope trick"—ask her about it, but plan to be tied up all afternoon while she shows it to you. Monday through Friday the coffeehouse is open from 11:00 A.M. to 2:00 P.M. and, on Thursday and Friday nights, from 6:00 to 11:00 P.M.; Saturday it's open from 11:00 A.M. to 11:00 P.M. Call (501) 623–0653.

To get an overview of the town, go up to the 216-foot Hot Springs Mountain Tower in the national park. Taking the glass-enclosed elevator to the open-air deck is a treat. But from the top of West Mountain, there's an equally good view; you can even see the tourists in the tower on the other mountain. The view is especially pretty at night. Pull your car off on the turnouts and enjoy the scene below—downtown Hot Springs glittering like the fabled spa it once was.

Going down from West Mountain onto Prospect Street, you will see a Russian villa at 634 Prospect. The fairy-tale house is vivid in red and yellow, with intricate decorations on the detailed shutters in the style of a northwestern Russian summer home, or dacha. It was designed and built by a former officer of the Czar's army in 1930. Once abandoned, the house is now owned by Adam Roberts, who operates English Tailors. Roberts and his wife lived in England, where they acquired the tailoring skills and the classic design sense of fine British clothing. A member of the Guild of Master Tailors there, he has recently received permission from the guild to make women's skirted suits as well. Custom-made suits, tuxedos, blazers, and even golfing plus-fours at a surprisingly reasonable price are designed and made to fit you perfectly. Roberts was trained as a designer and offers a complete personal design service, from sketches to finished clothing. Designs are sent to England, where the suits are hand-tailored of English fabrics and some Italian silks—with about 600 fabrics to choose from. Finished garments take about six weeks; American-made custom shirts are also part of the design. Design prices range from $464 to $1,000, and measurements can be done at the villa or at your hotel. Call for a free consultation: (501) 321–0963.

A longtime feature at Hot Springs is Dryden Pottery, located at 341 Whittington Avenue and offering pottery made of native clays and crystal quartz. Craftspeople like Tony Larson, a potter who is a former street artist, now demonstrate hand-thrown wheel pottery and explain each step. The showroom is filled with examples of the finished product. A mural painted on the building tells the story of the Indians and their pottery. Dryden is now listed in the *Antiques and Collectibles Price Guide* for its one-of-a-kind original pieces. Call (501) 623–4201 for hours and tour information.

There are several B & Bs in the Hot Springs area. If you want to stay in town, Pinewood Cottage Bed and Breakfast, at 119

Russian Villa Hot Springs

Pinewood, is an interesting place where Jack Chapman and Bea Tharp share their home with travelers. Jack calls himself a Yankee (he's originally from Mackinac Island, Michigan); Bea calls herself an "Arkie" (she's from the Heber Springs area); and together they have created a B & B in the true sense of the word. The cream-colored brick home, described as "gingerbread deluxe" by Bea, is trimmed in two shades of blue and wine, with stained glass and flowers everywhere. The home is built on a slope so that both of the two upstairs bedrooms and the bedroom on the lower floor have outside entrances, and there is plenty of privacy on the lower floor. A private bath, twins, and a queen-size hide-a-bed will accommodate the entire family.

The country kitchen has a brass wood stove where the proprietors share homemade snacks before bedtime and give you real down-home victuals for breakfast. The home is furnished with fine antiques, and Bea has made quilts for each bedroom. She whips up a full breakfast of just about anything, from blueberry pancakes to French toast, served in the sunny dining room or screened porch. Rooms are $40 to $45. Call (501) 624–3646 for reservations.

Hot Springs Country Club Golf Course is open to the public. Its tree-lined fairways and hilly forty-five holes draw golfers from all over the five border states. Midwesterners vacation here in February and March, when the weather is usually golfable but snow still covers the rest of middle America. (The fact that it's racing season doesn't disappoint anyone, either, if the weather is less than perfect.)

Stillmeadow Farm, 5 miles south of Hot Springs (the hub of this vacation area) on Scenic Highway 7, is a detailed reproduction of a New England saltbox, with post and beam construction that Gene and Jody Sparling designed and built on seventy-three acres so that guests can roam unhampered. A fire in the parlor greets guests on chilly nights. Breakfast is served in the dining room, where a walk-in brick fireplace is hung with dried herbs from the garden. Upstairs there are two bedrooms with private baths and a suite with a bath. At night the sound of tiny frogs on the pond (Gene calls them "peepers") lull guests to sleep. Gene is an accomplished wood-carver, and many of his detailed figures can be seen around the house. Rooms cost from $45 to $80 at the farm, which is located at 111 Stillmeadow Lane. Call (501) 525–9994 for reservations. The adjacent Sassafras Shop, also owned by the Sparlings, has a fine collection of antiques for you to browse among. The

Sparlings moved the shop from Hot Springs to the farm a few years ago, and the hours are variable. To find the farm and shop, go 5 miles east of Hot Springs on Highway 7; then turn east on Highway 290 and go about 1.5 miles to the sign.

Nearby on the same piece of property is **Mountain Brook Stables,** at 107 Stillmeadow Lane, where you can take guided trail rides in the Ouachita Mountains. Sunrise and sunset rides and day trips for both experienced and inexperienced riders are available. The Spaldings' son Gene and his wife, Deborah, own the stable, which houses eight horses and two mules. The animals are gentle and well broken. A one-hour ride, which costs $10, crosses a stream and climbs a small mountain path through a hardwood forest to the summit, from which Lake Hamilton and downtown Hot Springs can be seen. The longer, three-hour ride, which costs $25, starts over the same trail but turns into a hardwood and pine forest to follow the stream to a gorge, where riders stop to rest by a waterfall before the ride back over a different route. The stable is open from March into December, with rides offered from about 9:00 A.M. to about 7:00 P.M. Call (501) 525–8393.

The **Mid-America Museum** is situated in a heavily wooded, twenty-one-acre site about 6.5 miles west of Hot Springs off Highway 270 West. The 50,000-square-foot building is divided into two wings connected by a glass-enclosed catwalk over a stream. This is a hands-on museum, where the exhibits are designed to be touched. Here the arts and sciences come together with playful contraptions like the "Featherstone-Kite Open-Work Basketweave Mark II Gentleman's Flying Machine"—the work of Rowland Emett, who designed the mechanical creations in the movies *Chitty-Chitty Bang-Bang* and *Those Magnificent Men in Their Flying Machines.* The lighthearted tone of the museum delights visitors.

The museum's new Fine Arts/Science Program will rotate original works by internationally renowned artists, such as the globular pop-art abstractions and brightly colored geometric images of Italian artist Benini, with the works of sculptors who are Arkansas natives. Cross the bridge to the west wing and explore exhibits in perception, energy, matter, and life, each display showing the connection between the arts and the sciences. The "Balance Challenge" alters your equilibrium with mirrors, the "Walk-in Camera" allows you to see how a camera lens views the world, and the "Sun Scale–Earth Scale" shows how much you'd weigh on the sun.

The Laser Theater uses laser beams and music to create a thirty-minute show featuring Led Zeppelin's "Stairway to Heaven." There's even a life-size mastodon like the ones that roamed the Ozarks 18,000 years ago. Hours are from 9:30 A.M. to 6:00 P.M. daily Memorial Day through Labor Day and from 10:00 A.M. to 5:00 P.M. Tuesday through Sunday the rest of the year. Tickets are $3.95 for adults and $2.95 for children and seniors. Call (501) 767-3461 or, in state, (800) 632–0583.

Southwest of Hot Springs on Highway 70 is Springwood Farms Thoroughbreds in Pearcy. The place is more than just a thoroughbred ranch, however. Charles and Heidi Cunningham are also the powers behind **Second Chance Farm,** a nonprofit group that investigates and prosecutes cases of equine cruelty. Abandoned, starved, or just plain mistreated steeds (not just thoroughbreds) are taken in—horses that would otherwise be slaughtered or sent to the proverbial glue factory. Along with the effort to aid mistreated horses of various breeds, another program rehabilitates thoroughbreds that can no longer race. These animals have any necessary surgery, are retrained, and are offered for adoption to families who have the proper facilities to care for the magnificent horses after their racing days have ended. All stallions are neutered before adoption; mares are available for a lifetime lease, a foster home, or outright adoption. Please call ahead (501–767–5252) if you want to visit the farm and see some of the fine horses that call it home, so that someone can be there to show you around. Because the organization is nonprofit, donations are appreciated from those who care about the work being done here.

The drive along Scenic Highway 7 is the most beautiful way to travel south in this part of the state. "Birders" especially seek out this area because DeGray Lake Resort State Park near Bismark hosts many events for bird-watchers. Night owls will like **The Owl Prowl** on Friday and Saturday nights in summer (and in January); this event lets you see and hear barred owls, screech owls, and great horned owls by using taped calls to attract them. The annual Eagles Et Cetera in January is a weekend offering numerous opportunities to see bald eagles in the wild. You will learn how to identify birds or how to photograph them with some of the best birders in the state. The hour-and-a-half tour by barge—which can be chilly—offers more than a 95 percent chance of seeing bald eagles. The barge runs year-round on weekends and seven days a week from spring through fall. Tickets are $3.50 for adults and $1.75 for children ages six to twelve. Call (501) 865–4501 for information about the events.

The Eagle and Raptor Rehabilitation Program has these birds in temporary captivity, too. Other bird hikes continue throughout the day. Some other wildlife you might see include the common loon, great blue heron, raccoon, and gray and red foxes. All programs at the lodge and bird hikes are free, but advance registration for hikes and barge tours is necessary because of limited space.

There are other special events here, too. March has early-morning bird walks and the Easter Ecstasy spring wildflower walks (and annual Easter Egg Hunt). April's wildflower walks join the Tell a Tale Troupe Dinner Theatre, performing such classics as *Red Badge of Courage*. And Full Moon Cruises are available from April through October.

Reservations at the ninety-eight-room lodge should be made by calling (501) 865–4591 or (800) 633–3128. Lodge rates start at $51.00 for double occupancy; campers are charged $5.75 for water and electrical hookups and a dump station, with bathhouses containing hot showers also available. The park, which is located off Highway 7, 6 miles north of I–30 at Caddo Valley (21 miles south of Hot Springs), also has an eighteen-hole golf course, a pro shop, and a marina.

Scenic Highway 7 ends at Bismark, but if you take Highway 67 South through the Caddo Valley beginning at Malvern, the picturesque, 20-mile stretch will take you by a number of antiques shops (one in a town's restored train depot), a restored antebellum cabin, a petting zoo, and an old-time general store with woodcrafts and smoked meats. Highway 67 is the old route to Texas; if you want to get off of I–30, this is the way.

The shrill cry of a peacock might get your attention on Highway 67, where George Lateana, an aviculturist, and his wife, Angela, raise both game birds and wildlife, as well as exotic birds and animals, at the **Feathered Nest Wildlife Farm,** 7 miles south of Maivern. An Australian black swan floats on the pond among the white mute swans. There are also emus, rheas, and pheasants to watch (many are touchable). George has been raising animals for most of his life, and according to Angela, when they married, the pygmy goats and such came with him. The couple has lived here since "retirement" about nine years ago, and Angela now creates unusual gifts that are sold in the gift shop—decorated eggs, crafts, and crystals, as well as one of the largest displays of Tom Clark's gnomes in the state. Hours are from 10:00 A.M. until 6:00 P.M. Tuesday through Saturday all year. Call (501) 332–3563.

The area around here is a rock hound's dream; Magnet Cove on Highway 270 East near Malvern is said to have one of the country's most varied deposits of rocks and minerals. It is named for the magnetic iron deposits in the area.

The city of Malvern has such historical attractions as the Boyle House Museum and the Rockport Bridge. From Malvern take Highway 171 west past Lake Catherine State Park. This park has seventeen cabins. Some are rustic single units where on chilly evenings you can enjoy a warm fire in the stone fireplace; others are modern duplexes. They are situated on a little peninsula on the lake, and most are on the lakeshore; the price is $50. But if you want to try your hand at roughing it, Rent-a-Camp provides tents, cots, a stove, and other camping equipment. When you tire of grilled hot dogs and the traditional chocolate-and-graham cracker "s'mores," a modern park restaurant overlooking the lake is open during the summer season. Call (501) 844–4176 to make reservations.

The Ouachitas

Built along the bluffs of the Ouachita Valley, Arkadelphia was a river port during steamboat days. Now it calls itself the Wildflower Capital of Arkansas, and acres of them have been planted along the roadways and on public land. Take home a T-shirt saying GROW WILD IN ARKADELPHIA! The town has two universities literally across the street (and a ravine) from each other—Henderson State University and Ouachita Baptist University—and this arrangement has created one of the country's more interesting rivalries; their fierce athletic competition is legendary. Ouachita Baptist houses the personal library and memorabilia of Senator John McClellan, and Henderson State has a museum housed in a wonderful antebellum home featuring relics of the Caddo Indians. Both campuses are lovely, with huge oaks and interesting architecture.

Something Special, at 2503 West Pine Street, is where Becky Bost and Connie Mitchell make paper angels (similar to cornhusk dolls) that began as a hobby and became a business. The angels are shown at the War Eagle Fair and exported to shops in other states. The tree-topper, at 20 inches tall, costs $17.50; the doll-size angel, at 10 inches, costs $10.50; and the ornament-size angel costs $7.50. The shop also carries other handmade natural decorative accessories—grapevine wreaths, arrangements using all-natural dried flowers, herbs, and seasonal decorations. It's open on Monday, Wednesday, and Friday year-round with the exception of mid-September through Christmas, when the shop is open Monday through Friday and often on Saturday. To make an appointment anytime, call (501) 246–7544.

Arkadelphia is unofficially the peanut brittle capital of the state—there are three shops located all within 1 block of one another, all good. The original one, **Glover's Candy Kitchen** at 1224 Walnut Street, opened twenty-one years ago and is famous for its red and white striped buckets of peanut brittle. This is owner Bill Glover's mother's recipe, made in small batches and stretched by hand. The recipe is a secret. No preservatives or salt is added. This crunchy nut treat comes in buckets because it is so doggone irresistible. Call (800) 748–9524 or (501) 246–8921 to order some. The shop is open from 8:00 A.M. to 5:00 P.M. year-round but stays open until midnight during the busy season, which is from October until after Christmas. If you want to taste-test first, Juanita's and Andrew's are the other two shops nearby.

Highway 67 rolls into Gurdon, where the **International Order of Hoo-Hoos Museum** will answer the questions of the curious about the history of the Supreme Nine, who handle the business affairs of the International Order of Hoo-Hoos. Ever wonder about the history of the Snark of the Universe, called the Supreme Hoo-Hoo, leader of eight other directors—the Senior Hoo-Hoo, the Junior Hoo-Hoo, the Scrivenoter, Bojum, Jabberwock, Custocatian, Arcanoper, and the Gurdon? Want to know more about the State Deputy Snark and the Viceregent Snark? You can get all the details here. "What's a Hoo-Hoo?" you ask. People in this timberland know. It's a fraternity of lumbermen—its symbol an arching Egyptian black cat with its tail curled into the number 9—and it was formed to foster "elbow-rubbing" and the spirit of teamwork and is dedicated to health, happiness, and long life for its members. The museum is at 207 Main Street. Hours are 8:30 A.M. to 5:00 P.M. Monday through Friday (it's closed at noon for lunch). Call (501) 353–4997.

The wooded rolling hills along Highway 53 south from Gurdon

eventually lead to **White Oak Lake State Park,** 725 acres of timbered hillsides. Here in the hardwood forests, the Beech Ridge Trail offers a glimpse of the Gulf Coastal Plain. The gentle trail is 2 miles long and takes you from the thick underbrush of the edge of the woods into the shaded forest floor where life abounds. As the elevation drops, the pines of the uplands meet the lowland hardwoods, where the Caddo Indians lived some 200 to 300 years ago. Boardwalks cover the bottomland part of the trail to protect the unusual plants that live in this moist soil. Orchids grow here—in the early spring the twayblade orchid and later other orchids and arums (such as the jack-in-the-pulpit) are seen here.

A bridge takes you across the stream where the soil is mostly white sand, the remnant of an ancient shoreline that was formed as the Gulf of Mexico receded from the area more than a million years ago. The fine white sandhills lead around a slight curve and ascend into the sand barren, an isolated spot where the soil is infertile and few plants can survive—but the ones that do are unique to these zones. Riddel's spikemoss, for instance, looks like little sand castles and, like moss, dries up and waits for rain to revive it and release its spores. But unlike moss and more like fern, it has roots and, like pine trees, has a conelike megaspore. It is unique to the sandhills and is sort of a "missing link" between lower and higher plant levels. Call (501) 685-2748 for information.

There used to be quite a number of ferries across the many rivers of Arkansas. Bridges and freeways have done away with most of them, however; only three are left in the state. One of them carries cars across the Red River on Highway 160 in the southwest tip of the state. If you plan to be out that way to visit the Conway Cemetery Historic State Park near Walnut Hill, you might enjoy the ride across the river; then you can sing "Remember the Red River Valley" with more meaning. The park is dedicated to the memory of James S. Conway, the first governor of the state. The half-acre family cemetery where the governor is buried is on the eleven-and-a-half-acre site, which also contains the governor's plantation home, Walnut Hill. Take Highway 29 to Bradley and then Highway 160 west for 2 miles to Walnut Hill. Turn left on the county road and proceed 0.5 mile to the park entrance. No camping or visitors' services are available.

Texarkana: The name of the town is derived from TEXas, ARKansas, and LouisiANA, which borders nearby. Photographer's Island, at the front entrance steps of the post office, is a spot where you can photograph yourself standing in two states at one time. Scott Joplin, the "King of Ragtime Composers," grew up here; a colorful outdoor mural depicts his life, a must-see stop.

Before the coming of the settlers, the territory around Texarkana was the Great Southwest Trail, for hundreds of years the main line of travel between the Indian villages of the Mississippi Valley and those of the West and Southwest. The Great Caddos tilled rich fields and fished and hunted along the Red River, where they raised maize, beans, pumpkins, and melons.

In the 1850s the builders of the Cairo and Fulton Railroad pushed through to meet the Texas and Pacific Railroad here. One of the first town lots sold here in 1873 now houses the Hotel McCartney. Quite a few of the really interesting things are on the Texas side of the line; there is a walking-tour map available that will lead you to many of them.

Razorback fans blanket the state. They don't all hang out in Fayetteville, because the Razorbacks have some of the most loyal fans on the planet. In this state people pack any stadium where the Hogs are playing. They wear various hog emblems to football games, and thousands of red-shirted fans chant the praises of the fierce-snouted, tusk-brandishing razorback.

It's almost a religion, and **Hog Heaven,** Gordon Buckworth's place at 308 Arkansas Boulevard, is where you can buy any razorback item you can imagine. It has everything—yes, everything, from umbrellas to toilet seats—with the infamous razorback emblazoned on it. Not only is the razorback the university's mascot, but the local high school has been razorback country even longer than the university. So if you want a T-shirt, a necktie, a poster, or anything else with the almighty hog on it, visit Hog Heaven. Hours are from 9:00 A.M. to 6:00 P.M. Monday through Friday and from 9:00 A.M. to 5:00 P.M. on Saturday. Call (501) 772–4647.

Established in 1824, the town of Washington was, for more than fifty years, the jumping-off point for the unknown Indian Territory and Texas, a welcome sight for travelers on the Southwest Trail. The trail was an old Indian path and an important route for settlers, stretching diagonally across the territory from Missouri to Texas and forming part of the trail that 3,000 Choctaw Indians traveled when they were forcibly evicted from Mississippi and sent to Oklahoma on the well-known Trail of Tears.

Old Washington Historic State Park is a timewarp back to those days. Like Williamsburg, it's an authentic re-creation—as authentic as modern restoration and archaeology can make it—of a frontier boomtown of the 1850s. The entire town of Washington lies in a state park. Private homes are mixed with historic structures in the 1-square-mile area, along with the state's largest and most magnificent magnolia tree. The narrow dirt roads were laid out almost 160 years ago when thousands of people were headed for Texas and stopped at the hotels in town to buy supplies. Davy Crockett, Sam Houston, and Stephen F. Austin passed through Washington headed west. During the Civil War Washington served as the Confederate capital after Little Rock was captured by the Union army in 1863.

A blacksmith shop stands on the site of an earlier shop, and inside the glowing metal is still fashioned by leather-aproned men who hammer out knives like the first bowie knife, designed here by smithy James Black for Jim Bowie. Today people travel from great distances to learn the ancient art of knifemaking at one of the world's few schools of bladesmithing, classes sponsored by Texarkana College and the American Bladesmith Society. The shop is open year-round.

Spring brings splashes of yellow jonquils scattered over the hillsides, along roadsides, and in flower boxes all over the city to celebrate the annual Jonquil Festival in the middle of March. The quiet town of 265 is inundated with visitors, more than 40,000 at last count, who come to see the bright display of flowers, some of which are descendants of bulbs planted by the pioneers—as are the aging, gnarled catalpa trees that shade the gravel streets. During the festival craftspersons carve walking sticks of sumac, make brooms of straw with antique tools, or weave rugs on looms. Bowie knives are displayed in the park's gun shop, which also contains a seventeenth-century Chinese matchlock gun, muzzle-loading rifles (demonstrated by costumed traders in town), and a German machine gun from World War II.

The Pioneer Cemetery is filled with pre–Civil War tombstones. Small markers dot the area where wagons bogged down in the bottoms of the Saline and Ouachita rivers and where attacks by Rebel troops at Poison Springs, Marks Mill, and Jenkins Ferry killed 700. All these can be seen on the walking tours of the town—tours that take about two hours and begin at the 1874 Hempstead County Courthouse, which houses the park's visitors' center. There are plenty of other sights visitors can explore on their own, too. A printing museum shows the evolution of printing during the nineteenth century; the B. W. Edwards Weapons Museum contains a collection of more than 600 weapons; and the Black History Museum, housed in a doctor's office built about 1895, portrays the important role black Arkansans played in the history of Washington.

Williams Tavern Restaurant, now operated by the park, began as a "stand" on the road, an open house where, for pay, John W. Williams entertained travelers. It was one of the best-known spots between Memphis and the Red River. Today the menu is posted on the blackboard and features such homemade specialties as chicken and dumplings, potato cakes, and apple cider. Hours are from 9:00 A.M. to 4:00 P.M. The Pioneer Grocery also serves sandwiches. And nearby Tavern Inn re-creates the feeling of the pioneer era: The bar has an antique brass rail, and pre–civil War bottles line the shelves, just as in frontier days.

There are several Greek Revival homes, among them the Royston House and the Sanders-Garland Home. At both places women in period dress check their hoopskirts in the petticoat mirror before greeting visitors. The Royston home towers behind huge magnolia trees, and flowers line the dirt drive leading up the hill to the front door, which has stained glass windows depicting the four seasons. (Looking through one blue-paned glass makes things appear as though a blanket of snow were on the ground.) The house is filled with Empire furniture. The L-shaped, 1845 Sanders-Garland house has a large back porch where the family spent warm evenings. A portrait of daughter Sara hangs over the fireplace. A third house, The Dr. James Alexander Purdom home, circa 1850, features exhibits on early medicine.

The Confederate capitol of Arkansas (from 1863 until the end of the Civil War) is open to the public, as is the 1874 red brick courthouse. For those interested in serious research, Washington is also the home of the Southwest Arkansas Regional Archives (SARA), dedicated to collecting and preserving source materials for the history of the area. SARA is in the Old Washington Courthouse and can be used by all serious researchers, including grade-school students. Although materials cannot leave the archives and must be used in the research room, copies can be made of most materials in good condition. The park is open year-round from 9:00 A.M. to 5:00 P.M. daily. Admission is $4.00 for adults and $2.00 for children. Call (501) 983–2684.

Another unique state park lies north of Washington on Highways 4 and 27. If diamonds are a girl's best friend, then women have a lot of pals around Murfreesboro—not in the quaint town square but in nearby **Crater of Diamonds State Park,** because there diamonds not only are forever but also are practically free. These are not phony "diamonoids." They are the real thing, *and* this is the only—repeat, only—diamond mine on the North American continent. There is a $3.50 charge to enter the digging area, but after that anything you find is yours to keep. Yes, diamonds are free here; all you have to do is pick them up. It's finders, keepers no matter how valuable they are, and almost 1,000 diamonds are found every year—the average is three a day. More than 60,000 diamonds have been found in the eighty-acre crater. It's tricky; all that glitters is not diamonds. But here's a secret that makes this book worth the cover price: Dirt won't stick to diamonds like it does to other rocks, according to Jim Cannon, park superintendent. And most diamonds are found in kimberlite breccia, which is a greenish rock. The gems are said to be from 95 million to 3.1 billion years old. Diamonds come in yellow, brown, pink, and black. And even if you don't find diamonds, you may find other semiprecious stones, such as jasper, opal, agate, quartz, amethyst, and garnet. There is even a geologist on the park staff to verify the gems; gems are identified and weighed for you. The 40.23-carat "Uncle Sam" diamond is the record, but the 34.5-carat "Star of Murfreesboro" and the 15.31-carat "Star of Arkansas" wouldn't make a bad piece of jewelry, either. They are among the biggest, and they whet the urge to dig for most visitors.

The diamonds should be all gone by now, you say? Wrong. Geological forces push the diamonds upward slowly through the kimberlite soil, and the park plows the crater occasionally to increase the chance of bringing them to the surface of this 35-acre field, which is the eroded crust of an ancient volcanic pipe. The park is on Highway 301 about 2 miles southeast of town and is open daily from 8:00 A.M. to 5:00 P.M. Call (501) 285–3113.

Murfreesboro is a real gem (you should excuse the pun) of a town. It is just northwest of the park on Highway 301. Every Saturday night during the summer, there is free entertainment at 8:00 P.M. in front of the Conway Hotel, which also has a flea market and an outlet for the art and crafts of local artisans. The hotel is on the National Register of Historic Places.

The Queen of Diamonds Inn is on Highway 26/27, 1 block

north of the square. Al and Jane Terrell bought the house and renovated it a few years ago, managing to combine Victorian charm and modern convenience. The office is in the 1902 home, which is filled with authentic furnishings. Motel rooms were built behind the home, and guest rooms there are new and modern. A complimentary continental breakfast is served in the cheery breakfast room in the house. Rooms cost $44.50; call (501) 285–3105 for reservations.

The **Ka-Do-Ha Indian Village** is near town, about 1.5 miles off Highway 27 on Caddo Drive. It is the site of a prehistoric Indian settlement—home of the Caddo Mound Builders—and many artifacts are on display. The village is a combination archaeological-dig-and-museum. You can tour the mounds and hunt for arrowheads on the surface, but state laws prohibit digging. The mounds are in fields surrounded by woods; they are open, although some greenery has grown up around them, and you can see the remains and artifacts. An article about the mounds appeared in *Archeology Today Magazine,* but as yet the mounds are relatively undiscovered by tourists and there are no great crowds here. The gift shop and the Happy the Prospector gemstone mine are here, too, selling bags of rough minerals you can take to the water sluice and wash for your own gemstone. Hours at the village are from 9:00 A.M. until 5:00 P.M. in winter and until 6:00 P.M. in summer every day. Admission is $3.00 for adults and $1.00 for children. Cliften and Faye Crews are the managers; they offer a wealth of information about most places around town. Call (501) 285–3736.

Miners' Village in town also has a Happy the Prospector shop and sluice, this outlet also offers sixteen flavors of hand-dipped ice cream. Hours are Tuesday through Saturday from 9:00 A.M. to 5:00 P.M. The shop and sluice are uptown on Highway 27 North: Go west from the courthouse square for 1 block and follow the yellow signs. Caddo Antiques, also on the square, is one of those places that have it all: antiques, rare and used books, baseball cards, and furniture. Hours are from 9:00 A.M. to 5:00 P.M. Monday through Saturday. Call (501) 285–2719.

Diamond hunting isn't the only outdoor activity that glitters near here. The Little Missouri River flows clear and cold and is the home of possibly the best fly-fishing for rainbow trout in the state. It is also home to the scrappy smallmouth bass that provide some of the best action for sport fishermen. The tailwaters below the dam are icy, and you can fish from a canoe or flat-bottom boat or just wade in and do it the old-fashioned way. If that experience has made you happy, continue north about 9 miles on Highways 27/70 to Glenwood, where you will find the Caddo River—a beautiful, spring-fed stream full of those same smallmouths. It is floatable year-round, and canoes and guides are available in Glenwood for pack-in trips in the wilderness. Crawfish is the bait of choice.

You can see why fishermen favor this part of the state. Daisy State Park, in the foothills of the Ouachita Mountains near the northern end of crystal-clear Lake Greeson, is famous for its thirty-pound, "lunker-class" striped bass, northern pike, and walleye. Above the lake on the Little Missouri lurk fighting rainbow trout, too. But this park has something more: It caters to motorcyclists with the 31-mile **Bear Creek Cycle Trail,** on the west side of the lake. The trail goes to Laurel Creek and is open to motorcycles, all-terrain vehicles (ATVs), and nonmotorized bikes as well, although if you are pedaling, a mountain bike would be a good choice, for this is a 31-mile *one-way* trip and it's mountainous. ATVs are not allowed in the park except on the trail. There's a parking lot at the trailhead to offload your ATVs, and motorcycles can be driven to the parking lot by roadway. The trail and park are open year-round seven days a week. Call (501) 398–4487.

In October the bike tour from Daisy to Crater of Diamonds Park 23 miles away is an annual event. There is an entry fee, but you get a free T-shirt for the tour. An interpretive program of guided hikes, games and crafts, and evening slide and movie shows in the park's outdoor amphitheater are free during the summer. Campsites have electric and water hookups but half of the twenty-one tent sites are for hike-in camping only. The clear waters of the Caddo River begin their path to the sea in the Ouachita Mountains near Mena, and the Caddo Valley is ideal for camping in primitive campsites on the abundant sand and gravel bars. From the town of Daisy on Highway 70, go 0.25 mile south. Call (501) 398–4487.

Highway 369 meets Highway 84 after it goes north from Highway 70 and the park. **Country School Inn** on Highway 84 in Langley is owned by Eddy and Charlotte Ayers, who have converted an old stone schoolhouse in the foothills of the Ouachita Mountains into a homey bed-and-breakfast. The seven bedrooms are converted classrooms—very large—and the school gym next door is open to guests. Dorm-style rooms for groups and family-style rooms are available. The lounge and dining area is the former auditorium, and the stage is now the kitchen. Each room is decorated with comfortable country and antique furnishings. Even a merry-go-round and swings can still be found on the playground, along with grills and picnic tables, with wood provided for cooking. A full breakfast is served every morning. Rooms are $28; call (501) 356–3091 for reservations (the schoolhouse is closed in January).

Two beautiful sights in this region are the 4-mile Winding Stair portion of the Little Missouri Trail and the **Little Missouri Falls** near the Albert Pike Campgrounds north of Langley. You have to hike in to see them, but they are *almost* accessible by road via a short (0.2-mile) hike from a picnic area with parking. The falls are a series of 10-foot stair-step falls in an area designated as "wild," meaning that all roads into the area are barricaded and closed year-round. This walk is still a bit of a tester for older people because of about 25 yards of steps. But the trail winds along the river and through rocky, tree-shaded canyons, and the only sounds are the rocks kicking up riffles and the birds and squirrels chittering in the trees. Or, if you are still feeling your oats, you can camp at Albert Pike and hike 6.3 miles along a trail of short-leaf pine, old-growth American beech trees, American holly shrubs, and plenty of white oak, hickory, and red cedars—a trail that parallels the Little Missouri River to the falls. The trailhead is at Forest Service Road 106, a good dirt road, 2 miles from the Albert Pike Recreation Area. Watch for the Forest Service emblem marking the trailhead.

The falls are only 6 miles from the headwaters, and the river is not wide at this point. The trail fords the river at the southern end and crosses a creek near the northern trailhead, so some wading is required. The falls are between Round Mountain and Hurricane Knob. To drive to the picnic area from the Albert Pike Campgrounds, go north on County Road 73 about 2 miles; then take a left turn on County Road 43 and go about 5.5 miles, taking County Road 25 to the left for 1 mile and County Road 593 to the left about 0.25 mile. There are five picnic tables there, as well as parking. Be sure to take your camera or sketch pad.

If you prefer a canoe or kayak, the river is peaceful and shallow and lazes along in summer, looping around wide gravel bars, forming deep swimming holes and rock towers. After spring rains, though, the Winding Stairs portion of the river is crooked and

Little Missouri Falls

steep and capable of producing Class III rapids after a big storm: not easy to navigate for beginners.

East of Langley on first Highway 84 and then Highway 4, you can meet **"Beauty and the Beast"** if you are in the mood for danger and adventure. "Beauty and the Beast" is what they call the Cossatot River, and 11 miles of the most rugged and spectacular river corridors pass through Cossatot River State Park near Wickes where Highway 4 meets Highway 71. The river begins in the Ouachita Mountains southeast of Mena and rushes south for about 26 miles into Gillham Lake. The waters are the home of two fish found only in the southern Ouachita: the leopard darter and the Ouachita Mountain shiner. The park covers more than 4,200 acres of wooded slopes and cascading clear water. There are Class III, IV, and V rapids on this wild-running river, thus making it a favorite with rafters, kayakers, and canoeists. They say that Cossatot means "skull crusher"; the river can be dangerous. It flows over and around upended layers of bedrock, sometimes dropping 60 feet per mile, and contains narrow valleys and lengthy rapids and falls. The river is not recommended for the inexperienced; it is called "probably the most challenging" white water in the state.

How's that for understatement? Call (501) 385–2201 for information about the river.

Mena is where Highway 71 runs into Scenic Highway 88. The city is in the shadow of Rich Mountain. The newly restored, 1920 Kansas City Southern Railroad Mena Depot Center, at 514 Sherwood, is a combination museum-and-visitors'-center. It houses the Mena Chamber of Commerce, a tourist information center, and railroad displays and memorabilia. Quality crafts from a 60-mile area are for sale inside. The center is run by community volunteers who know their way around the area quite well.

The **Ansata Arabian Stud Farm** is a working farm showcasing world-class Egyptian-Arabian horses 13 miles west of Mena on Highway 8 West. This breeding farm belongs to Don and Judi Forbis, who'll arrange a tour of the facility any day but Sunday. The Egyptian-Arabian is a smaller-boned, more refined Arabian, with a more dish-shaped face, used for halter-class and western pleasure-class showing. These fine animals are bred for endurance and are popular for trail rides. The farm has eighty to one hundred horses on 450 acres. Visitors can see both breeding stallions and the show-string horses—the travelers of the farm. Office hours are 9:00 A.M. to 5:00 P.M. Monday through Friday; call (501) 394–5288.

Highway 88 shows off the 54 miles of twists and turns along **Talimena Drive** as it winds along the crests of forested mountains between Mena and the Oklahoma border, within the boundaries of the 1.6-million-acre Ouachita National Forest, covering almost all of Montgomery County. The drive spans the highest mountain range between the Appalachians and the Rockies. Getting off the road is full of pleasures, too. Hiking trails wind through the forests along ridges, lakes, and streams. It's a heaven for nature lovers. The area is one of America's oldest landmasses, and the rock there tells the geologic history of the area. At the crest of Rich Mountain stands a historical fire tower 2,681 feet above the valley.

Rising high above the clouds on Rich Mountain, **Queen Wilhelmina Lodge** in the state park of the same name, was destroyed by fire in 1973 and rebuilt in a style that reflects its past, with stone fireplaces, comfortable rooms, and a spectacular view; it is perched on the highest elevation in the park on steep and winding Highway 88. The first lodge was built in 1896 by the Kansas City, Pittsburg, and Gulf Railroad and was designed as a retreat for passengers on the line. The 3-story lodge became known as the "Castle in the Sky" and was named for Holland's young queen (there was largely Dutch financing for the lodge). A royal suite was set aside for her in hope that she would decide to make an official visit someday, but she never did. Dining in the lodge's restaurant gives you a view above the clouds.

Other attractions in the park include a small railroad, miniature golf, camping, and an animal park with creatures to pet. The state park is 13 miles northwest of Mena on Highway 88, but in bad weather it is advisable to take Highway 270 to Highway 272 and then to go south for 2 miles; continuing west takes you to the Pioneer Cemetery historical marker before crossing the state line into Oklahoma. Call (501) 394–2863 or 394–2864 for lodge reservations.

Talimena Drive crosses Highway 259 and begins to climb along the spine of the Winding Stair Mountains. There are several interesting spots along the drive: Billy Creek Recreation Area, Emerald Vista (which has not only camping but interpretive and equestrian trails), Lake Wister, Cedar Lake Recreation Area, Horsethief Springs, and Old Military Road historical sites all perch on the ridge of the mountains. You will have a sweeping view of the Poteau River Valley.

Highway 88 east from Mena leads to the only town in America named after a radio show—Pine Ridge. If you are old enough to remember radio days and are at all nostalgic about it, first close your eyes and listen to your memories and then open your eyes and take a look at Dick Huddleston's **Lum and Abner Museum,** or the "Jot 'Em Down Store." Is it the way you thought it would be? You will never see Fibber McGee's closet. You will never see the Shadow ("Who knows what evil lurks in the heart of men?"). But this musuem is on the National Register of Historic Places, and you can walk right in and let your imagination soar. Arkansas natives Chester Lauck and Norris Goff, better known as Lum and Abner, entertained listeners during the 1940s with a radio show filled with down-home humor, and today the store looks just as it did, or how we imagined it looked, back in the 1940s—an old potbellied stove near the post office window in the general store (with the museum situated in the next room). You can call (501) 326–4442, and although neither Lum nor Abner will answer, postmistress Kathryn Stucker will.

If you have followed Highway 88 east, you will be entering an area called the "Quartz Crystal Capital of the World," and there are several commercial mines around here. **Wegner Quartz Crystal Mines,** 3 miles south of Mount Ida on Highway 27, are perhaps the only mines where you can find your own crystals. The mines are open year-round from 8:00 A.M. to 5:00 P.M. seven days a week. You don't have to dig very deep to find crystals in one of the three mines. The digging fee ranges from $6.00 to $20.00 a day, and you can keep what you find. Tim, the manager, says that finding a crystal is almost guaranteed. One of the mines is a hike in—0.25 mile up a mountain slope, a strenuous walk not recommended for older people—but you can be driven to the other location (in Tim's pickup truck), where you can dig in the red clay until you find all the crystals you want. The six-sided, single-point crystals are the most common and can be clear or cloudy quartz. The clusters are more difficult to find; they require more work and some luck, too. Crystals range in size from a quarter of a pound to ten pounds. Richard Wegner, owner of the mines, also has showers and campsites available near the retail area, which is 3 miles south of Mount Ida on Highway 27. Call (501) 867–2309.

Some nice side trips to resorts and picnic areas can be found along Highway 270. This beautiful part of the state offers scenic drives worth exploring for an afternoon or for a weekend. Premier among them is the twisting drive to the summit of Hickory Nut Mountain that leads to a panoramic view of Lake Ouachita and its many islands. This region is remote and natural with small towns sprinkled throughout the hills. It is a fine place to escape the hustle of the city life and enjoy the beauty of the Natural State.

Off the Beaten Path in Southeast Arkansas

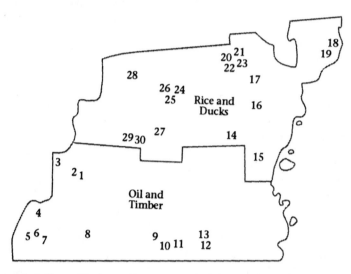

1. McCollum-Chidester House
2. Art Academy
3. Reader Railroad
4. Logoly State Park
5. Lois Gean's
6. Slingin' the Paint
7. Georgia's
8. Weyerhaeuser Company Reforestation Center
9. El Dorado
10. Arkansas Oil and Brine Museum
11. Felsenthal National Wildlife Refuge
12. Wiggins Cabin
13. Trieschmann House Bed and Breakfast
14. Miller's Mud Mill
15. Japanese-American Relocation Center
16. Arkansas Post County Museum
17. Bullock's Lodge
18. Delta Cultural Center
19. Edwardian Inn Bed and Breakfast
20. Pickett's Soul Food
21. Cajun Hid-Away
22. Stuttgart Agricultural Museum
23. Arts Center of the Grand Prairie
24. Arkansas Railroad Museum
25. Mrs. Jones' Cafe
26. Margland II
27. Pioneer Village
28. Grant County Museum
29. The Klappenbach Bakery
30. Wynne Phyllips House Bed and Breakfast Inn

Southeast Arkansas

Several of the counties of southeastern Arkansas share the Ouachita River, but high bluffs, unspoiled forests, and the river bottoms give each area a distinct personality. If you enjoy gentle currents, a float on the Ouachita, with your fishing gear, is perfect.

In the early 1700s French trappers encountered the Ouachita Indians living in small villages on the banks of the river. *Ouachita* is the French way of spelling the Indian word, which sounds like "Washita," but the meaning of the word has been lost—perhaps "good hunting," or "river of many fish," some say.

This is where the timberlands begin, after the Ouachita Mountains, on the way to the Mississippi Delta. The timberlands are where the Gulf Coastal Plain and the Arkansas River Delta meet, too. This lush area, covered with vast forests of southern pines and drained by sleepy bayous and sloughs, is a favorite with sports enthusiasts because of the exceptional fishing and hunting it provides.

The longest bayou in the world, Bayou Bartholomew, meanders through the timberlands. The history of the country is seen from a southern view in this part of the state, and plantations and antebellum homes dot the Mississippi bottomland along the mighty river.

Oil and Timber

Camden stands on a bluff at a horseshoe curve of the Ouachita River. The Quapaw Indians, a branch of the Sioux, were friendly to early Spanish explorer Hernando de Soto when he made his trip up that river in 1541. The distance is 5 miles around the river's bend but less than a quarter-mile across the neck of the curve. In fact a man named Woodward once set more than a hundred slaves to digging a bayou, which, had it been completed, would have become the main channel of the river, leaving the town sitting high and dry on the loop.

Camden is an old Deep South city where cotton bales once lined the streets leading to the wharf. A varied collection of restored antebellum homes, including the circa 1847 **McCollum-Chidester House,** at 926 Washington Street NW, attests to this heritage. This house, which is haunted (more about that in a moment), w s used as headquarters by Sterling Price, a Confederate general, and Frederick Steele, a Union general, during the battle of Poison Springs in April 1864.

The house is filled with the original furniture and even has some bullet holes in the plastered walls of an upstairs room where stagecoach drivers slept: Union soldiers shot at stagecoach driver Colonel John T. Chidester—who had allowed Confederate soldiers to read Union mail he was carrying on his stagecoach—as he was hiding in a secret room near the stairwell. A pair of crystal hurricane globes, a mahogany and walnut secretary, and a sewing machine date back to 1850, along with Mrs. Chidester's needlework and clothing. The original dining table is set with Mrs. Chidester's silverware and china (which were buried under a tree in the yard to keep them safe from Union soldiers). The east bedroom is haunted by an apparition of a man dressed in a long coat, carrying a cane or sword. It appeared reflected in a mirror in a photo taken by a member of the historical society in 1985; copies of the photo can be purchased here.

The historical society has built a carriage house in the backyard. Since this was a stagecoach stop, a replica of one of Chidester's Concord stagecoaches and a turn-of-the-century surrey are parked there. The home is open April through October from 9:00 to 4:00 P.M. on Wednesday through Saturday. Admission is $3.00 for adults and $1.00 for students. Call (501) 836–9243.

The Confederate Cemetery, at the junction of Adams Avenue and Maul Road, less than a mile from town, is the resting place of the more than 200 unknown young men killed here. It has many other interesting stories of the lives and times of the early settlers. Beautiful examples of the almost-forgotten craft of wrought iron work appear in fences around many plots. One unusual grave site contains only four weathered posts and a heavy iron anchor chain connecting them. It is said to be the grave of a child who died on a steamboat trip. The boat stopped only long enough to bury the little girl, and the crew used what it had on board to mark the spot.

The **Art Academy** at 251 Adams Avenue NW is the studio and gallery of artist Kathryn Marino. The cream and blue home was built in 1891, originally as a church; in the 1920s it was made into a home; and since 1985 it has been a gallery and learning center as well as an art supply store. One room of the academy is filled with Kathryn's work—mostly oils, with some watercolors and

113

Reader Railroad

acrylics. Another room is a gallery showing the work of other recognized artists in the area. The rest of the house is dedicated to teaching aspiring artists of any age, and a resource center is filled with Kathryn's large collection of art books used in her classes. Artists from other media hold workshops in the Marino studio. Gallery hours are from 10:00 A.M. to 5:00 P.M. Monday through Friday. Call (501) 836–7355.

Venture down Highway 24 to Highway 368 and make the 3-mile loop to the steam-powered **Reader Railroad** near Reader, which rolls down the "Possum Trot Line" through forestlands on the oldest standard gauge railways in North America. In 1887 the St. Louis, Iron Mountain, and Southern Railway constructed a line south from Gurdon through Camden to El Dorado. It cut through an area of virgin timber and sawmills, and logging lines followed. From Memorial Day through late October, this full-size train with a wood-burning steam locomotive takes you through an ever-changing landscape from the old mill town of Reader to Camp DeWoody, a logging campsite. Call (501) 337–9591 for schedules.

Logging trucks rumble down the highways, and trucks stacked high with chicken crates cruise in a confetti of feathers: Forestry and chicken ranching are the main businesses as you head south. But along Highway 79 between Camden and Magnolia, you'll see what is perhaps not the most *beautiful* of yard ornaments (but better than a birdbath)—oil wells—gracing lawns.

Six miles north of Magnolia on County Road 47, just off Highway 79 near the McNeil Highway junction, is **Logoly State Park.** This is not pronounced to rhyme with "by golly"; rather it sounds more like "Low-ga-lie." The name has nothing to do with the Loblolly pine, either. It is actually an acronym of the names of three families who gave the land to the state—the Longinos, the Goodes, and the Lyles. The park has medicinal waters bubbling up in eleven natural springs in the forest; people once traveled from far away to drink and bathe in the mineral waters. Logoly was also the state's first environmental education park, and observation stands and photo blinds dot the trails for nature observers and bird-watchers. The mineral springs and unique plant life make it worth exploring.

The visitors' center houses exhibits of the park's history and natural environment. Summer hours are 8:00 A.M. to 5:00 P.M. daily; winter hours are 8:00 A.M. to 5:00 P.M. Monday through Friday and 1:00 to 5:00 P.M. Saturday. Call (501) 695–3561.

South of Camden on Highway 79 lies the city of Magnolia. As the name tells you, flowering trees grace this city's landscape. The courthouse is surrounded by them, and fragrant blossoms burst into bloom just in time for the Magnolia Blossom Festival, art show, and steak cook-off the third weekend in May. Courthouse Square is a direct copy of the square in Oxford, Mississippi. The original Tiger Harry's (with great Tex-Mex food favored by the college crowd from Southern Arkansas State University) is in the Best Western Coachman Inn at 420 East Main Street, 3 blocks off the square. The restaurant was named after Harry, the son of the original owner, who was, well, "rambunctious," according to locals.

The motel is a typical Best Western, an old-style colonial plantation building complete with pillars, but it has something no other motel has: a bright black touring coach with cranberry red leather seats, drawn by a matching team of proud Belgian horses. Ray Sullivent, owner of the inn, takes great pride in the coach and the town. The driver of the coach tells stories of the fine old homes on the thirty-minute route. The carriage top folds down on fine summer nights or pops up to display a cranberry red fringe. Call (501) 234-6122 for information about the carriage, which usually runs Thursday through Saturday from 6:00 P.M. to 9:00 P.M. (or until dark on long summer nights).

There is also a hayride around town the third Saturday of every month, followed by an old-fashioned country music show started locally and housed in an old furniture store that now has a stage. It's called Union Street Station (501–234–6010) and owner Randy Lann draws a crowd from far and wide.

Shopping for exclusive designer clothes, something in the $200 to $1,200 price range? Then stop by **Lois Gean's** at 109 South Jackson. The shop is listed right there with the high-dollar department stores in *Vogue* magazine as the place to buy designer clothes. The ad says, "Lois Gean's, Magnolia," with no state mentioned—because people "in the know" know where Lois Gean's is. People who shop for Donna Karen, Escada, and Ann Klein clothing and who like Valentino bags and Judith Leiber accessories shop here and have come from miles around to do so for forty-three years. Lois Gean's started as a small gift shop and has bulged sideways to take in 4,400 square feet of the neighboring buildings. The rustic entrance, with its cast-iron stove and old brass mailboxes, belies the polish inside, and dynamic owner Lois Gean Kelly travels to New York on buying trips to keep the shop *au courant.* Call (501) 234–1250. The shop is open Monday through Saturday from 10:00 A.M. to 5:00 P.M.

If that is too pricey for you but you still want something exclusive, find **Slingin' the Paint,** at 102½ North Washington downtown on the square. Ceil Bridges's hand-painted, one-of-a-kind garments are also carried in the big-name department stores, but they are made right here in Magnolia and have been seen on the televisions shows "Designing Women" and "Evening Shade." T-shirts, dresses, pants, bags, ties, accessory pieces, and children's clothes are all made here, and you can come in and watch them in the various stages of completion. High-quality work, all done by hand, is what has made the business expand out of Ceil's home, where it began, and into 5,000 square feet of work space. Prices start at $60. Hours are from 9:00 A.M. to 5:00 P.M. Monday through Friday; call (501) 234–8776.

Georgia and Tommy Snider's restaurant, **Georgia's,** at 2630 Columbia Fifteen (at Burnt Bridge Road), is in the house built in 1944 for Tommy's grandmother, a house built with lumber cut off the land itself; the original well and bucket are still on the back porch. The roomy house, with its L-shaped porch, is 6.5 miles outside of town on four acres of crepe myrtle and pines. Entering the house, you will be startled to see a huge carved bedroom suite with a bed so tall that it almost touches the 9-foot ceilings. That's just the beginning, because all four dining rooms are filled with antiques. The Sniders serve catfish, shrimp, smoked pork ribs, and steaks—the couple won the annual steak cook-off with their secret recipe of herbs and spices one year. But the homemade rolls and fried pies are the specialty. Fruit pies, raisin pies, and coconut or chocolate cream pies are top sellers. Yes, you read that right: a fried chocolate cream pie.

There's a map on the wall in one room, and people from all over the country have marked it. At last count only Montana, Maine, and "a couple of those little states on the east coast" were not marked. So if you are from one of those states, get over there and sign in. Call (501) 696–3942 for reservations.

The **Weyerhaeuser Company Reforestation Center,** just outside of Magnolia on Calhoun Road, is where fifty million seedlings a year are born from some 600 parent trees. The people at Weyerhaeuser know the ancestry of each tree ("It's sort of a stud farm for trees," says Lester Hutchins of the Magnolia Chamber of Commerce) and have chosen the area because the environment is perfect for reproducing pines. The birth and upkeep of these native trees are a full-time job in this timberland. In the spring seeding operations can be seen; in the summer the seedlings grow, covering the acreage with a soft green fuzz; in the fall cone harvesting and processing go on; and in winter seedlings are harvested to sell to both forest products companies and individuals in a five-state area. Although southern pine predominates, other trees—different kinds of oak and some cypress—are grown in the forest. Respect and care for the environment are demonstrated in this area, despite the logging that sometimes strips hillsides bare before they are replanted. This is an environmental education stop worth a visit. Two videos are available: The first shows the birth and growth of the trees grown here; the second relates the life cycle of the forests. To find the forest, go south on Highway 79 to the first intersection (less than 1 mile), turn east onto Calhoun

Road, and proceed about 6 miles to the center. Call ahead at (501) 234–3537; group tours can also be arranged.

Driving east on Highway 82 brings you to the city of **El Dorado.** In 1921 the town prospered when black gold began gushing and the sweet smell of crude oil pumping onto the land and into the once-pristine waters of the Ouachita River drew the get-rich-quick crowd of promoters, drillers, roughnecks, and thieves. The town filled with itinerant oil workers, and the population jumped to 30,000 persons who needed to be fed. A 3-block area called Hamburger Row sprang up. Now, some seventy years later, more sophisticated restaurants line the street, and the city is not to be missed if good eating is high on your list of "things to do while traveling."

Most of the buildings downtown were built in the boom days when oil flowed freely from the wells around here. Now one of two "Main Street" cities in the county, El Dorado has been restored, and brightly colored awnings, pear trees, and park benches have been added to the old lampposts that line the streets. The place boasts handsome old homes and the South Arkansas Arts Center. The old Union County Courthouse on the town square, the heart of the community, is a massive, neoclassical building containing more columns than any other structure in the state. The Rialto Theater, at 117 East Cedar on the square, has also been restored and is the state's only working art deco theater, with gilded, vaulted ceilings and waterfall curtains.

You can spend a lot of time walking the downtown square. Hear the tinkle of a player piano? It's coming from the Smackover General Store, 211 East Main, where Becky Isbell offers an intriguing blend of arts and crafts, antiques, food, and more. This is truly a "nook-and-cranny store" chuck-full of goodies. But mainly, the shop caters to collectors with an extensive choice in collectibles. There are Fontanini figurines made in Italy, Martha Holcolmb's All God's Children figurines, East Texas Pottery from Marshall, Texas, Tom Clark's gnomes, and Christmas decorations year-round. Hours are from 10:00 A.M. to 5:00 P.M. Monday through Saturday. The coffee pot is always on for visitors. Call (501) 863-3123. Next door at 209 East Main is an antiques mall and above that is a second floor gallery featuring the work of local artists.

La Bella Gourmet Gifts and Delicatessen, at 119 North Jefferson, features delicious sandwiches, soups, meats, cheeses, and salads, as well as gift baskets. It is also well known for its cinnamon rolls and powdermilk biscuits. It's open Monday through Saturday from 8:00 A.M. to 7:00 P.M.; call (501) 862–4335.

Tiger Harry's Restaurant, at 117 East Main Street, is where water comes in quart mason jars with a wedge of lemon and a straw. You're going to need it, too, because a note on the menu says, "We put jalapeños on just about anything—just ask," and they do. A neon sign over the kitchen announces WE BE COOKIN'; a giant red neon Pegasus adorns the bar (where Rattlesnake Beer and Rolling Rock Beer are sold); and friendly waitresses let you sit back and relax. Trying to finish the half-pound Tiger Burger with *jalapeños,* cheese, tomato, and a huge load of spicy, unpeeled, steak fries is a real test of your eating capacity. But even more challenging is an order of the Deluxe Nachos—chips covered with sour cream, guacamole, beans, meat—enough to feed a family of five. "No one has ever finished them," the waitress said. Desserts include Mug Pie, a hot fudge pie in a mug topped with ice cream or Crispitos, and apple- or cherry-filled burritos, deep-fried and served with ice cream. Call (501) 863–6611. Hours are 11:00 A.M. to 10:00 P.M. Monday through Thursday and 11:00 A.M. to 11:00 P.M. Friday and Saturday.

The Old Towne Store, at 113 North Jefferson Street, is a bakery and bulk food shop offering foods prepared only with natural ingredients—homemade soups and sandwiches (with whole grain breads) and freshly baked pies and pastries. Owen and Twila Guengerich are Mennonites who understand what words like *fresh* and *natural* really mean. The aroma of baking bread and cookies fills the shop. Mrs. Guengerich describes the store as the source of joy in her life, and profits from it go to such causes as African orphanages and the World Missionary Press. Hours are Monday through Saturday from 9:30 A.M. to 6:30 P.M.; call (501) 862–1060.

But even though it's tempting to spend the day on the square, the rest of the city has some surprises, too. There are plenty of antiques shops and restaurants tucked around town. If you are not on the square at lunch time, you might search out the old Mahony home at 303 East Peach Street. There, about a dozen years ago, SAAC Lunch was opened. It is owned and staffed by the South Arkansas Arts Center, and all profits go to the education program there. Volunteer help and the menu change daily. The lunch selections include such favorites as cannelloni, salmon croquette, seafood in shell, and California chicken breast. The restaurant is open Monday through Friday from 11:00 A.M. to 2:00 P.M. and serves wine and beer. Call (501) 863-7228.

Smackover, north of El Dorado on Highway 7, is worth a side trip because it is the other "Main Street" city in this county. The name comes from nearby Smackover Creek, which got its unusual name from the French explorers who found the banks of the creek to be covered with sumac and so named it *Sumac Couvert.* (Sumac couvert soon became pronounced "smackover.") "Boomtown Murals" are painted on the facades of the stores alongside Kennedy Park on Broadway Street; 1923 was a time when oil and money flowed freely and the town was prosperous.

The **Arkansas Oil and Brine Museum,** located 1 mile south of the oil-rich town on Highway 7 Bypass, is surrounded by twenty acres of woodlands. Six operational exhibits are on site, including a working oil well, pumping rig, and three derricks. And surprise! There's an art gallery inside, too. Stop first at the information desk in the lobby for pamphlets describing the indoor and outdoor exhibit areas. Temporary and traveling exhibits are displayed in the Exhibition Center, with two video presentations depicting the discovery of oil and brine in the state. No admission fee is charged to see the machinery and equipment that made this area explode in the 1920s, when the Busey Number 1 oil well blew in. Notice the colorful murals by Phillip Grantham that depict the history of the oil boom. Videos, tapes, and transcripts of oral histories of the roustabouts and roughnecks who lived and worked in the boom era are available to the public. A gift shop in the museum offers a variety of unique gifts related to the petroleum industry and the 1920s.

The Smackover oilfield was the largest in the country for a five-month period in 1925. Oil Field Park, the outdoor portion of the exhibit, has a 1920s standard rig and a 112-foot wooden derrick, the tallest known wooden derrick structure in the country. There's a spot to picnic, but if you want to see the real thing, you can get a tour through the forty-acre Smackover Field, just north of the museum, with acres of salt flats where the oil pioneers disposed of salt water that came from the ground, along with the oil from when the oceans covered the southern part of the state. The museum, located at 3853 Smackover Highway, is open Sunday from 1:00 to 5:00 P.M. and Tuesday through Saturday from 9:00 A.M. to 5:00 P.M.; call (501) 725-2877.

Returning from Smackover, then driving east from El Dorado north on Highway 15, is one of the more scenic drives in the southern part of the state. The 14-mile-drive from Moro Bay to Hermitage is a tranquil journey on a good county road. Houses along Highway 15 are a mixture of Victorian and modern styles. There is a free ferry to whip you across the Ouachita River by Moro Bay State Park (ferry hours are from 5:00 A.M. to 10:00 P.M. daily); it's one of only three free ferries left in the state. This is where Moro Bay and Raymond Lake join the Ouachita River.

If you decide to go southeast from El Dorado on Highway 82 between El Dorado and Crossett, you will be passing through the **Felsenthal National Wildlife Refuge,** which has a visitors' center off Highway 82 at Grand Marais. Lifelike dioramas show the 65,000-acre Ouachita River bottoms with wildlife, native plants, hardwood trees, uplands, and permanent water. In the Native Inhabitants diorama, an archaeologist (an animated mannequin) unearths ancient artifacts and tells the story of Native Americans from the Felsenthal Basin. The Saline River flows from the Ouachita foothills to the Ouachita River at the wildlife refuge, and here you'll find the world's largest green-tree reservoir—home to such rare species as the red-cockaded woodpecker, the bald eagle, and alligators—as well as good bass fishing. Call (501) 364-3168.

Crossett, on Highway 82 east of Lake Jack Lee, is a former sawmill town started by a lumber company in 1903. It has a multifaceted gem of a city park, containing a 3-mile paved hiking trail circling Lucas Pond—a quiet little lake stocked with bass and crappie for fishing—cutting through thick woods filled with honeysuckle and grapevines, and ending near the zoo, which has alligators, wolves, and peacocks. East of the pond in a wooded setting is **Wiggins Cabin,** circa 1800—the oldest building in Ashley County. The cabin was restored by the Crossett Cultural and Historic Society. Area senior citizens fired bricks and split cypress boards for the roof. The old house, a square-hewn cypress log dogtrot (containing two living areas under one roof, with a breezeway between), shows the labor of a man skilled with a whipsaw, broadax, and adze. Broadax marks scar the logs, and beveled horizontal lathes were used to fill spaces between the box-notched logs. The cabin dates from the settlement's earliest days in the "Great Wilderness" of towering cypress, canebrakes, and rattan vines of the Bayou Bartholomew. Today it looks as though someone lives there, right down to the strips of fabric trailing from a rocker onto the floor, as if Mother had just stopped her rug-braiding to fix dinner.

Next door is the Old Company House, built before 1910 by the Crossett Lumber Company for its employees. It, like all the other company houses, was painted "Crossett Gray," one of the cheapest paints sold at the time. It, too, looks lived in. A "four-eye" wood-burning stove stands in the kitchen with a pancake griddle and teakettle. Nearby is a washtub used for everything from scrubbing clothes and bathing to cleaning hogs. A bare bulb hung in each of the three rooms. Tours for both may be arranged by calling the Crossett Chamber of Commerce at (501) 364–6591.

The **Trieschmann House Bed and Breakfast** is at 707 Cedar in Crossett. Owner Pat Owens calls this a "laid-back sort of place." The house was a company house built in 1903, the same year the town was incorporated. But because it was an official's house, it was different and fancier than the other company houses around town. The 2-story white house has more than an acre around it. A breezeway and a large porch with ceiling fans and wicker furniture make the three-bedroom house a pleasant place to spend warm evenings. One of the bedrooms has a private bath ($35), and the other two share a bath ($30). A large family room with a fireplace and cable television for everyone's use is on the main floor. Mornings find folks gathered around the kitchen table for a full breakfast. Call (501) 364–7592 or 364–6901 for reservations.

Brown's Fish Market and Cafe, on Highway 52 North, started out as a fish market, but soon owners Buford Brown and his wife, Virginia, began cooking the catch and sending it out on plates. The next thing you knew, there were tables. Along with the Louisiana catfish, you can buy crayfish in the spring and Buffalo fish when it's available. Virginia makes hot yeast rolls, homemade pies, cakes, cookies, and hush puppies. The place is open from 5:30 A.M. to 8:00 P.M. Monday through Thursday and until 9:00 P.M. Friday and Saturday. Call (501) 364–2108.

The Georgia Pacific Corporation has gained national recognition for its tree-farming methods. The Levi Wilcoxon Demonstration Forest at Hamburg, north of Crossett on Highway 82, has three distinct types of forest, interconnected by a nature trail winding around Lake Georgia Pacific. The forest contains 250-year-old virgin growth, as well as pine seedlings and pine sawlogs more than 70 years old. Near the forest stands the giant Morris Pine—a loblolly pine tree 130 feet tall that measures more than 197 inches in circumference at its base. It is estimated to be more than 150 years old.

Lake Village sits on the west bank of an old oxbow lake called Lake Chicot, the state's largest natural lake, an enormous oxbow of the great river forming the eastern border of the state. Lake Shore Drive follows 18 miles of waterfront through the city; it passes a marker designating the spot from which Charles Lindbergh made aviation history with his first nighttime flight. Highway 65 is only 6 miles north of the Louisiana border, and the rich alluvial soil reaches a depth of more than 1,000 feet (the world average is 7 inches); this is prime cotton-growing area, and the Mississippi River, just a few miles from town, creates some beautiful scenery.

Rice and Ducks

Miller's Mud Mill pottery shop, at 15 Lennox in Dumas, north of Lake Chicot on Highway 65, is where Gail and Mitch Miller and their three grown sons, Mitch Jr., Matthew, and Carey, create hand-thrown stoneware pottery. Gail's trademark is a watermelon slice, appearing on plates and mugs all over the shop. Her popular line has been exported as far as Japan. Behind the shop four kilns are fired up, and on any given day you will usually find Gail working at the wheel. Out front, wind chimes, cookie jars, mugs, and all manner of neat things fill the shop, which is open from 8:00 A.M. to 6:00 P.M., "give or take," says Gail. Call (501) 382–5277.

A **Japanese-American Relocation Center** site at Rohwer, on Highway 1 off Highway 65 and near McGehee, was established September 18, 1942, by the federal government in the chaotic aftermath of the bombing of Pearl Harbor. Unique monuments remain here, built by internees at this relocation center where Japanese-Americans lived during World War II. The center is on the National Register of Historic Places but until lately hasn't received much attention. The people of McGehee, under the leadership of Mayor Rosalie Gould, are working to establish a museum to document and interpret the site. Sam Yada, a former internee who lives in Sherwood, leads an effort to build a new monument to honor those Japanese-American soldiers who were killed in action during World War II while serving in the U.S. military.

Today all that is left at the site is the cemetery, the monuments, and a brick smokestack. The monuments, exceptional works of sculpture built in 1944, show the fine artistic skills of the internees. One monument is dedicated to the Japanese-Americans from the camp who died while fighting for the U.S. Army in Europe; this monument is shaped like a tank, with a star-topped column rising in the center. Another monument is dedicated to those internees who died while in the camp; it features a column that is covered with elaborate Japanese script and is topped by a globe with an eagle perched on it. The simple concrete grave markers were also made by the people living in the camp. The museum is planned to show how relocation affected the lives of both the Japanese-Americans and the local people. The camp is about 12 miles north of McGehee on Highway 1 toward Rohwer. A sign on Highway 1 will direct you toward a gravel road leading to the site.

In 1673 two Frenchmen, Father Jacques Marquette, a Catholic missionary, and explorer Louis Jolliet, set out to explore the Mississippi Valley, traveling down the huge river from a French outpost on the north end of Lake Michigan to where Helena stands today. In 1682 they were followed by French explorer Rene Robert Cavelier de La Salle, who wanted to establish forts along the river. One of his officers, Henri De Tonti, stayed and established a trading post where the Arkansas and the Mississippi rivers converge.

Follow Highway 1 north from Rohwer to the Highway 65 intersection to find the **Arkansas Post County Museum** in Gillett. It marks the first permanent settlement in the lower Mississippi Valley. It was known as the Arkansas Post; homesteading began and, since the rich soil was perfect for cotton, was soon followed by slaveholding planters. Cotton became king. The main building is pioneer homestead–style, with an open fireplace in the kitchen, complete with cooking pots and offering a glimpse of how cooking and household chores were done. The Refeld-Hinman House, built about 1877 near Hinman Bayou, is an old log house that now serves as headquarters for the Arkansas Post State Park. The 1930s Child's Playhouse contains built-to-scale furniture and a wood-burning fireplace. The Peterson Building's early-life-style exhibits include one on pioneer washday, as well as depicting a country store and a farm workshop and displaying a vintage 1910 Stoddard-Dayton automobile. A gift shop is at the entrance to the

Arkansas Post National Memorial. The museum is open March through October, from 9:30 A.M. to 4:00 P.M. on Wednesday through Saturday and from 1:00 to 4:00 P.M. on Sunday. (In November and December it is open Friday to Sunday only, and it is closed in January and February.) Call (501) 548–2634.

The Arkansas Delta is land built by rivers and has its own special language for the lowlands—words like *levees, bottoms, backswamps, point bars,* and *oxbows.* When the practice of dueling was outlawed, the islands of the Mississippi were used as dueling grounds because they were out of the jurisdiction of lawmakers.

Hunters, of course, flock to this area just as the ducks do. The Mississippi flyway has a large number of hunting clubs and lodges, and when the season is right, they fill up fast.

Bullock's Lodge, on the banks of the Arkansas River at the Big Bayou Meto near DeWitt, offers down-home cooking and bunkhouse-style accommodations for up to fifty people for hunting duck and white-tailed deer. Billy Paul Bullock raises mallards from hatchlings to maturity and then releases them for controlled hunts, so the hunting is perfect for beginners or for training retrievers. Private rooms in the main house or bunkhouse are $200 a day, and the price includes breakfast, a light lunch, and a southern-style dinner.

The price also includes hunting "put and take" with the lodge's own mallards (so no license or duck stamp is needed) or wild hunting in green timber and flooded ricefields during the state's hunting season. "Put and take" hunting uses wild flying mallards, raised in a natural environment. Shooting is fast and tough as the ducks zigzag through flooded hardwood timber just as wild mallards do. The liberal season is October 1 to March 31.

Hunt clubs allow both individual hunting and group hunting, wherein you can analyze the day's shooting in the comfortable clubhouse or enjoy a game of snooker in the gameroom and bunkhouse-style accommodations. Bullock's guides will place you on your stands during white-tailed deer season. Talk to Louise Bullock or Judy Pettit for reservations (501–946–3509).

The Louisiana Purchase Historic Marker and State Park, at the junction of three counties east of Holly Grove, preserves the 1815 benchmark used to survey the Arkansas area of the Louisiana Purchase Territory. It contains about thirty-six acres within a headwater swamp, a fast-disappearing ecological setting in eastern Arkansas. A boardwalk provides access to the monument in the swamp's interior that marks the "point of beginning" for the survey. To find it from I–40 at Brinkley, take Highway 49 and travel 21 miles south to Highway 362; then drive 2 miles east on Highway 362.

Rising above a bustling Mississippi port, Helena is an old river town on the slopes of Crowley's Ridge. It is a town steeped in history, with antebellum, Edwardian, and Victorian homes and buildings scattered among rolling hills. Because of its position on the river, Helena was of strategic importance during the Civil War, when control of the river meant cutting the Confederacy in half. The Battle of Helena was one of the bloodiest in the state. The Confederate Cemetery on Holly Street contains a monument to the war dead and a panoramic view of the Mississippi.

Helena, founded in 1833, is Arkansas's major Mississippi River port and one of the oldest and most beautiful communities in the state. Here wharfboats once tied up indefinitely to the landings on the river, with every kind of store and concession on board. Dozens of offices on Water Street and on Ohio Street made it a busy area. The street nearest the river began to drop off bit by bit as the river ate at its shores, and many buildings were moved from Water Street to save them. Most of the caving in of the riverbank occurred just after the Civil War. Soon Cherry became the main street.

The **Delta Cultural Center,** at the south end of Cherry Street in the downtown area, is an outgrowth of the city's blues heritage and rich cover of topsoil left by the winds and rivers of the area. The visitors' center is in the Helena Train Depot, built in 1913, recently renovated, and now the home of the Cultural Center and Blues Museum. The building's arched windows and orange tile roof reflect the sunlight and sounds of the adjacent river. The museum contains exhibits of the changes in landscape and lifestyle of the Delta, with themes covering early inhabitants, the Civil War, and music of the region, using artifacts, music, and film. The gift shop offers handmade crafts, railroad memorabilia, and posters. A reconstructed houseboat porch lets you live the story of the "river rats" who inhabited the Black and White rivers. A caboose, with its railroad sounds and elevated navigation seats, gives kids a hands-on sense of the railroad era. The most popular portion of the center is the darkened corner room, where music flows from hidden speakers. The rough wooden floor and counter stools evoke the hard life and gritty work of the early inhabitants of the Delta. Photos and artifacts from the clubs of the city recall the blues legacy of such musicians as B. B. King and Sonny Boy Williamson and of the roadhouse bands of "rockabilly" favorites Conway Twitty and Charlie Rich.

An interpretive boardwalk to span the natural wetlands from the Mississippi River levee to the Helena Harbor is being built as the second phase of the complex concentrated along the levee. This winding, elevated boardwalk from the levee to the harbor opens the banks of the fabled Mississippi. Under way is a dock where riverboats from St. Louis to New Orleans will soon deliver passengers to the riverwalk. The center is at the corner of Natchez and Missouri streets at the harbor, at the end of the city's business district. Hours are from 9:00 A.M. to 5:00 P.M. daily, and admission is free. Call (501) 338–8919.

The area around the center is filled with shops and restaurants. Just across the way from the center is This Little Pig Antiques, at 105 Cherry Street. A nice shop for browsing, it has craft items, old silver, and antiques. It's open Monday through Saturday from 10:00 A.M. to 5:30 P.M.; call (501) 338–3501.

There are three historic districts in Helena, each with its own interesting sites and a fine collection of antebellum and Victorian homes and festivals celebrating the town's Deep South heritage. Tours of the homes and a downtown walking tour of the city are available from the Chamber of Commerce.

In *Life on the Mississippi,* Mark Twain said, "Helena occupies one of the prettiest situations on the river," and so it does. Hernando De Soto crossed the river here, followed in 1763 by Father Jacques Marquette and explorer Louis Jolliet. The city is filled with large modern homes as well as dozens of sturdy Victorians. Rolling hills, trees, and deep Bermuda lawns line the wide streets. This is obviously a town of old money.

The blues have played an important role in the American musical heritage of jazz, rhythm and blues, and rock and roll. Such greats as Sonny Boy Williamson, Robert Junior Lockwood, and Robert Nighthawk have been broadcast on the "King Biscuit Time" radio show on KFFA in Helena since 1941, and the King Biscuit Blues Festival is celebrated in October to commemorate it. But Helena is also the hometown of lyric soprano Frances Greer and country singer Harold Jenkins, better known as Conway Twitty.

The deep yellow **Edwardian Inn Bed and Breakfast,** at 317 South Biscoe Street, was built in 1904. It was the home of

Edwardian Inn Bed and Breakfast

William Short, a cotton broker and speculator who spent more than $100,000 in 1904 to build his family's dream house. The home contains eight original fireplace mantels, detailed woodwork, wainscoting, and paneling. It has unusual wooden floors of "wood carpeting" parqueted in Germany from strips of 1-inch-wide wood mounted on canvas and shipped to town in rolls. The huge wraparound porch is a fine place to rock on a warm afternoon. The building is one of the most interesting structures in this historically significant town and is on the National Register of Historic Places. Innkeeper Jerri Steed watches over twelve comfortable rooms: The home has nine rooms and three suites, all with private bath, phone, and television. A continental breakfast of homemade bread, cereal, fruit, and coffee is served in the cheerful, latticed sunroom. The cost is $45 to $50. Call (501) 338–9155 for reservations.

The sign on Highway 79 says WELCOME TO STUTTGART. Take the *t*'s out of the name and you have the word *sugar,* so it's called "Sugartown." Would you have figured that out? The town began in 1878 when a Lutheran minister born in Stuttgart, Germany, brought his congregation to the Grand Prairie region of Arkansas; nine years later the city was incorporated and named after the founder's birthplace.

Sugartown calls itself the "Rice and Duck Capital of the World." Farmers use the "flush and flood" method: Fields are covered with water just after planting to germinate the new seeds; it stands for a day or two. When the shrubby plants are about 6 inches tall, the fields are flooded and left underwater for the duration of the summer. Although rice does not need standing water to grow, the water serves as a weed control device. That's why ducks have always been plentiful hereabouts; the Quapaw Indians tied a decoy to their heads and submerged themselves up to the nose in the water among the cattails and weeds. When ducks landed nearby, the Indians grabbed the birds by the legs, clipped their wings, and took them home to a pen. As agriculture increased, the duck changed from "an acquired taste" to a tasty delight, since the birds started out eating wheat in the Dakotas, then dined on corn in Illinois, and finished up on Grand Prairie rice as they migrated south.

Duck is not the only food native to the Delta, of course. Part of the heritage of the Delta is the Afro-American culture brought with the slaves to this cotton country. For a taste of it, find **Pickett's Soul Food** at it's new home at 423 North Main for corn muffins and homemade pie. Harriett Pickett has been cooking in this neighborhood for ten years. Everything is homemade, and this is the place to try turnips and greens or sweet potato pie—food some call "ethnic" and others call just plain good cooking, foods most black Americans have known all their lives. Breakfast and lunch are served Monday through Saturday, and dinner is served Friday and Saturday; the restaurant is closed Sunday. Call (501) 637–6391.

The Deep South heritage also has its roots in Cajun cooking. Here's a place that's tricky to find but well worth the effort if you are cravin' Cajun: the **Cajun Hid-Away,** where Ann Prislousky and Lou Franks have been cooking up some of the best gumbo and red beans you're gonna find in the Delta area of Arkansas. Although the restaurant is in the process of moving to a new location, it's worth searching out, because shrimp are butterflied by hand and carefully breaded to fry, and the gumbo and other Cajun delicacies are mighty fine, too. The restaurant opens at 5:00 P.M. Tuesday through Saturday and stays open until 10:00 P.M., "or when everyone has been fed," says Ann. So call (501) 673–1833 for new directions to the restaurant.

Life wasn't easy for farmers on the prairie. But when the chores were done and they put the hoe down, they knew how to have fun, too. The **Stuttgart Agricultural Museum,** at 921 East Fourth Street (at Park Avenue), depicts the history of the pioneers who farmed the Grand Prairie of eastern Arkansas from the 1880s until 1921. You can see how they worked and how they played. The first families came to the area under the 1862 Homestead Act. An 1880 home is beautifully furnished from the era. A rustic prairie home and scaled-down reproductions of actual stores once here on the prairie—a mercantile, a doctor's office, a photography shop, a millinery, a grocery store, a post office, and, of course, the jail—are all part of the intriguing outdoor displays. The area was settled by German Lutherans, and the museum has a lovely little church, a two-thirds-scaled replica of the one that existed in the settlers' day. A minitheater lets you see the modern-day view from the cockpit of a crop duster's plane.

Famed wildlife artist William D. Gaither created realistic scenes for wildlife in its natural habitat, and the museum offers taped information on the flora and fauna of the Grand Prairie. The museum is open Tuesday through Saturday from 10:00 A.M. to noon and from 1:00 to 4:00 P.M.; Sunday hours are from 1:30 to 4:30 P.M. There is no admission fee, but donations are accepted. Call (501) 673–7001.

The **Arts Center of the Grand Prairie,** at 108 West Twelfth Street, provides rotating exhibits of local and state artists' paintings, sculptures, and other artwork. Not only is it a year-round exhibit, but other art-related activities are going on here all the time. Performing arts are presented, too. The Backporch Players, a community theater group, has several productions a year. A musical production runs in conjunction with the Grand Prairie Art Council's annual Grand Prairie Festival of the Arts. There is no admission charge to the center, and it's open from 9:00 A.M. to 5:00 P.M. Tuesday through Friday. Call (501) 673–1781.

South of Stuttgart on Highway 79, Pine Bluff, the second oldest city in the state, was founded in 1819 by Joseph Bonne, a French-Quapaw Indian, who built a log cabin on a pine-covered bluff overlooking a bend in the Arkansas River. Pine Bluff is now a trade center of the southeastern part of the state. It's a pretty town, with big old houses and wide streets. The University of Arkansas at Pine Bluff is here, and those interested in black history will enjoy the "Persistence of the Spirit" exhibit, which chronicles the lives of black Arkansans from pioneer days to the present.

Engine 819 and the **Arkansas Railroad Museum** at the Cotton Belt Railway Shops re-create railroading in the 1940s. The forty-seven-year-old engine was the last 4-8-4 steam locomotive ever built and was donated to the city by the railroad. This major restoration project, "The Pride of Pine Bluff," utilized all-volunteer labor, and now the train makes excursions for special events. You can see it at the museum, and, if you are lucky and your timing is right, you might even be able to ride on it. It travels to Fordyce each spring for the Cotton Belt Festival. You can call the Convention and Visitors' Center at (501) 536–7600 for more information about this beauty's schedule.

Highway 65 intersects with Highway 79 at Pine Bluff. **Mrs. Jones' Cafe,** on Highway 65 South, has been a favorite spot for years. Could it be the cornbread? Or perhaps the homemade pie? Or maybe it's because the cafe feels so comfortable, with its small tables covered with bright red and white cloths and with its white curtains letting sunlight through the square, white-trimmed panes of glass. Ruby Jones is still coming in every day to make pies (and she was eighty-nine at last count), although her family has taken over the rest of the work. A white basket on each table is filled with Ruby's homemade apple relish and apple jam, and the list of the current day's pies is on a chalkboard on the wall. *The Best of Ruby Jones* cookbooks are best-sellers here, as are the well-loved relish and jam. The present managers are Ruby's son W. R. Jones and his wife, Jan. Ruby's is open Monday through Saturday from 6:00 A.M. to 9:00 P.M. and Sunday from 11:00 A.M. to 2:00 P.M. for specials as tempting as chicken and dumplings, pot roast, fried chicken, and the daily turnout of some eighteen dozen rolls and biscuits to go with forty to fifty pies. All the vegetables are garden fresh, and the pies are, well, unique and wonderful: lemon pecan, egg custard, coconut cream, and sweet potato pie. The blackberry cobbler is a favorite, too. Call (501) 534–6678.

The Razorback wing of the Confederate Air Force, where everyone is a colonel (there is no other rank), has an annual affair the last week of August or first week of September. Then World War II trainers, fighters, bombers, and liaison planes are all there; it is like taking a step back in time, and the public is invited to take close-up looks at the planes. The air show is full of action, explosions, and fast-moving aircraft diving, turning, and smoking. Solo acrobatic acts, wing riders, parachute jumpers, and formation flights fill the skies. Call the Pine Bluff Visitor Information Center at (501) 536–7606.

There is a cluster of lovely B & Bs on Second Avenue in Pine Bluff. **Margland II,** at 703 West Second Avenue, is one of three homes owned by innkeepers Wanda Bateman and Ed Thompson. All three have been restored and decorated in an elegant fashion and serve as B & Bs. This one, a 1903 Colonial Revival house, is a Bermuda cottage of "shingle style" architecture and done in pastels—blue, mauve, and pink. The detailed beauty is filled with Victorian antiques and touches of the nearest holiday—Christmas offers particularly outstanding decorations. Three of the bedrooms have lofts. A large, modern kitchen at the back of the house overlooks the brick-paved yard, which has a gazebo and small wrought iron tables scattered about. The first floor and yard are used for private parties and wedding receptions. Rooms are $95, with "anything you want," states Wanda, for breakfast. It's a popular wedding and honeymoon spot.

Margland III is next door, at 705 West Second, and is done in a bold wine color scheme inside. Even the bathrooms are done in lovely detail. This structure was built as a duplex in 1894, and guests have use of the kitchen if they desire. Rooms are $50. Breakfast is included.

Margland IV, at 709 West Second, is a 1907 home with chambered projecting bays, round corners, and a porch with round corner turns. An exercise room, a whirlpool bath in each suite, and three loft bedrooms at the top of spiral staircases are part of the six suites, which all have private baths. Each is decorated with its own theme—country, art nouveau, Pennsylvania Dutch. A full breakfast is included, and other meals may be had by reservation. Rooms are $50.

And where is Margland I, you might ask? It's in the town of

Earle and was called Margland Farm. It's where Wanda Bateman's husband grew up. Call Wanda at (501) 536–6000 or 534–8400 for reservations at any of the three homes.

Pioneer Village, on Highway 35 in Rison, south of Pine Bluff, is a growing restoration of a village as it would have been during the last half of the nineteenth century. It includes Mount Olivet Methodist Episcopal Church, built in 1867 and containing handmade pews and many original windows; a 1902 country mercantile store selling handmade crafts, as well as homemade lemonade, 2-cent cookies, old-fashioned hoop cheese, and crackers; a doctor's simple Victorian home, built in 1892; Lois's Cottage, a two-room shotgun dwelling with a wraparound porch; and a one-room, circa 1900 log cabin with a fireplace for cooking and a handmade table for meals. A ladder on the cabin wall leads to the loft where settlers slept on straw mats. To the right of the cabin is the smokehouse and to the left a small herb garden. A fully stocked blacksmith shop, complete with anvil, bellows, and tools of the trade, is here as well, as is a barn with wagons and plows of the same time period.

The third weekend in March sees the dogwoods and daffodils in full bloom, and so this is the ideal time for the Pioneer Crafts Festival, when demonstrations of old-time crafts and string music fill the village. Original, handmade, quality items composed of native materials are for sale. (There is a small admission charge to the festival.) And on a Wednesday in the middle of December, a pioneer Christmas exhibit begins with carols in the church and ends, after dark, with an old-fashioned prayer meeting. The village Christmas tree, a tea table, and often a country supper fill the village with delightful sounds and scents. The mercantile is usually open from December 1 to 15 for Christmas shopping. For more information contact Rison City Hall at (501) 325–7444.

Modern archaeology buffs will make the drive to Sheridan, on Highway 270 west of Pine Bluff, because literally digging up the past is what Elwin Goolsby, the county historian and the founder and director of the **Grant County Museum,** is famous for. The museum, at 409 West Center Street (Highway 270), looks like an old mercantile store but is packed with things that preserve the history of the area. The retired history teacher has gathered thousands of historical items using a metal detector and a shovel. He and his team of amateur archaeologist—his students—have uncovered gas pumps made of solid iron dating from 1919; a rusted-out moonshine still, whiskey barrel hoops, and a lantern apparently smashed by ax-swinging feds in the 1930s; abandoned farming equipment; and 200 roadside signs. There are also musket balls, pistols, and scabbards from the Civil War. But probably the favorite items are the remains of a B-17 bomber that crashed in a swampy area north of town while on a training mission. The plane was left to sink into the bog, but when a road grader turned up a rusty pistol, Goolsby and his gang grabbed shovels and uncovered a machine gun, canteens, oxygen masks, and the dog-tags of some of the nine crew members who died there.

The museum area contains not only photographs and micro-film genealogical records but log cabins, barns, corncribs, and a depression-era church on the grounds. Each is filled with small items that tell a story—a tiny shoe from a little girl named Leola who died in a house fire; a slave's tombstone—reflecting the history of Grant County. An acre of ground about 1 mile from the sight, now called Heritage Square, is being used to save historic buildings scheduled for demolition. So far a Victorian folk house, circa 1904, and a small, 1927 cafe complete with kitchen utensils and dishes of food, have been restored. The museum is open from 9:00 A.M. to 5:00 P.M. Tuesday through Saturday; call (501) 942-4496.

Why is a county that lies in the heart of cotton country named Grant? Why is the county seat named Sheridan? They are named for two U.S. Army generals, Ulysses S. Grant (commander in chief of the Union army), and Phillip Sheridan, infamous Union cavalry leader, because the county was formed during the Civil War Reconstruction. Local folks blame the Yankee carpetbaggers.

Drive south of Sheridan on Highway 167 to Fordyce, which each spring celebrates its railroad industry with the popular, week-long Fordyce on the Cotton Belt Festival. Ole number 819, one of the few remaining steam locomotives in operation, rolls into town from Pine Bluff for rides. The childhood home of Paul "Bear" Bryant is a short drive from downtown on Highway 8; the football coaching legend grew up here and played football for the Fordyce Redbugs.

Smell the aroma of fresh bread in the air? You must be near the **Klappenbach Bakery,** at 108 West Fourth. The bakery turns out French, pumpernickel, rye, sourdough, cinnamon-raisin, and cheese breads, as well as oatmeal cookies, brownies, and muffins, all made from scratch by Norm and Lee Klappenbach. The bakery's reputation is so well known—all by word of mouth—that treats are shipped all over the country to people who came, saw, and were conquered by the huge selection of baked goods.

The bakery opens into the sandwich shop, where the proprietors' son Paul creates such mouth-watering sandwiches as the pepper steak cheese sandwich—grilled green peppers and onions, marinated beef sliced real thin, and melted swiss cheese, all on a poor boy bun fresh and warm from the bakery. There is always something hot—soup or quiche—and always-tempting desserts, such as cheese cake, meringue pie, a pastry, or chocolate chip cookies. The two dining rooms are quite large and filled with the Klappenbachs' eclectic collection of antique tables and cupboards in assorted sizes. The bakery and shop are open from 6:00 A.M. (for the doughnut crowd) to 6:00 P.M. Tuesday through Saturday and are closed Sunday and Monday. Call (501) 352-7771 to see what's cooking.

If you are staying the night in Fordyce, the **Wynne Phyllips House Bed and Breakfast Inn,** at 412 West Fourth Street, is one of the state's newest B & Bs. Agnes Wynne Phyllips and her husband, James, are the daughter and son-in-law of the original builder of this 1905 Classical Revival house. The large, tree-shaded lot has grape arbors for strolling, a lap pool for swimming, and lots of flowers. The house is furnished with family antiques and touches (like Oriental rugs) from the couple's travels all over the world. The four bedrooms with private baths on the second floor all have original furnishings. A mint julep on the front porch at night, if the mood strikes you, and a full southern breakfast, complete with grits and family-recipe biscuits, are part of the hospitality, and Agnes sends you to bed with a platter of homemade cookies, too. It doesn't get any better than this—and all for $55. Call (501) 352-7202 for reservations.

Off the Beaten Path in Central Arkansas

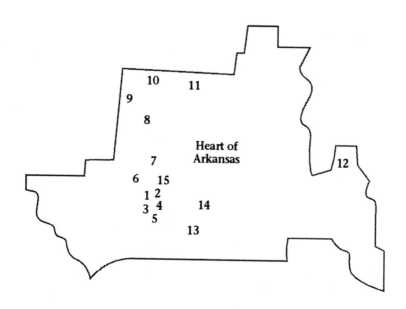

1. Dr. Witt's Quapaw Inn
2. Carriage House
3. MacArthur Park
4. Andre's
5. Cantrell Gallery
6. Ron Mynatt's Wood-
   carvings
7. Ouachita Trail
8. Pastimes Restaurant
9. Patton House Inn
10. Riddle's Elephant Breeding
    Farm and Wildlife
    Sanctuary
11. Hammons Chapel Farm
12. Great Southern Hotel
13. Toltec Mounds
14. Marlsgate Plantation
15. *The Spirit*

Central Arkansas

The Heart of Arkansas

The hub of the state is its central region. Here the capital, Little Rock, and its sister city across the river, North Little Rock are the core of the state's government, cultural, and financial life. Cosmopolitan and urban, the city and the suburban cities surrounding the capital offer sophisticated shopping, fine dining, and big-city nightlife.

Several state parks are nearby, too. Toltec Mounds, an archaeological site to the east, Pinnacle Mountain, an environmental education park—and trail head to the challenging Ouachita Trail—to the west, and Woolly Hollow State Park, north of Conway, can be part of your travel plans when you are based in the capital city.

Towns with names such as Pickles Gap, Toad Suck, and Romance dot the heart of the state, and there are surprises everywhere. There's a thirty-three room mansion on a plantation that is still growing cotton, and even an elephant breeding farm hidden away near this metropolitan center.

Start in Little Rock. It's called the "City of Roses" because of the abundance of the lovely flowers planted all over the city. Little Rock sits on a rocky bluff overlooking the Arkansas River. The best view of the river is from the walkways and terraces of seventeen-acre Riverfront Park at the foot of Rock Street. There the "little rock" for which the city is named is marked by a bronze plaque.

It's an interesting city for history buffs for it houses three state capitols, making Arkansas unique in this respect. The first, in the Arkansas Territorial Restoration at Third and Scott in downtown Little Rock (501–371–2348), represented the prestige neighborhood of territorial Arkansas: In a rough territory these 2-story brick homes with glass windows were solely for the wealthy elite. Huge old magnolia trees shade the area, and there is a feeling of leaving the modern world and returning to a different time. The Hindeliter Grog Shop, built in the 1820s, is the oldest house in Little Rock. Nearby are the Conways House, held together by white oak pegs and graced by original hand-carved mantels and doors; the 1820 Hinderlite House, constructed of large, hand-hewn oak logs and covered with red heart, hand-beaded cypress siding; and Federal-style homes with detached kitchens.

The second capitol, the circa 1836 Old State House at 300 West

Markham Street, is a perfect example of Greek Revival architecture, one of the most beautiful in the South. Six period rooms and a restored legislative chamber and governor's office, as well as changing exhibits, reflect nineteenth-century history. "Granny's Attic" offers a hands-on inspection of yesterday's toys, and a museum shop contains Victorian reproductions, crafts, and books. There is no admission charge. Hours are Monday through Saturday from 9:00 A.M. to 5:00 P.M. and Sunday from 1:00 to 5:00 P.M. Call (501) 371–1749.

And, of course, the new capitol, circa 1900—a downscaled model of the nation's capitol that is made of Batesville marble quarried in the state—finishes the list. Here the "Dash" bus sprints from the capitol to downtown for 25 cents, making lunch and shopping easy for both tourists and politicians. For information on tours of the building call (501) 682–1010.

Follow Seventh Street from the capitol to the Quapaw Quarter with its renovated Victorian homes and buildings. It extends from the capitol to I–30 and from the Arkansas River to Roosevelt Road and is an interesting place to spend the whole day. In fact if you want to stay the night, there are two B & Bs in the Quarter.

Dr. Witt's Quapaw Inn, at 1868 South Gaines Street, is in the Quarter's 1905, Colonial Revival Witt House in the Governor's Mansion National Historic District. Owners Dottie and Charlie Woodwind try to keep a homey place for visitors to the capital. Four fireplaces, pocket doors, lead glass windows that throw rainbows of light across the parlor, a wraparound front porch with plenty of comfortable chairs for enjoying early-morning coffee and newspapers—all add touches of quiet pleasure to this peaches-and-cream-colored home, which has four bedrooms, two with private baths. The price, $60 to $70, includes an expanded continental breakfast and features such touches as line-dried linens for guests, who have use of the whole house. Dottie even has a giant-screen television and a movie library. Call (501) 376–6873 for reservations.

There is only one other bed-and-breakfast in Little Rock, and that is the **Carriage House,** at 1700 Louisiana, in the newly restored carriage house that adjoins the 1891 home of Dr. Dan and Sandra Cook just 1 block from the Governor's Mansion. It has two bedrooms with private baths. Sandra serves afternoon tea and cookies in the courtyard, as well as breakfast in the main house. And what a breakfast it is—fresh fruit with Grand Marnier, French toast with Canadian bacon, or an herb omelet with homemade popovers and apple butter. The rooms are done in informal antiques and share a common sitting room downstairs. The price is $79. Call (501) 374–7032 for reservations.

Villa Marre, at 1321 Scott in the Quarter, is an elegantly restored Victorian built in 1881 by a saloonkeeper who wanted a little respect and had plenty of money to spend. He wanted a house that was elegant and would impress people with the refinement that seemed to be lacking in his profession. Combining Italianate and Second Empire elements and topped with a French mansard roof, the house contained indoor plumbing; its parquet floors of oak and mahogany quilt the floor with flowers, squares, fans, and zigzags. You may have already seen the arched windows and wrought iron fence of this lovely old home, for it appears on the television show "Designing Women." Villa Marre is open Monday through Friday from 9:00 A.M. to 1:00 P.M. and Sunday from 1:00 to 5:00 P.M. The phone number of the Quapaw Quarter Association is (501) 371–0075, and the organization offers a walking-tour brochure on other buildings in the historic district.

MacArthur Park, also part of the Quapaw Quarter, was the site of the Little Rock Arsenal, built in 1836. Here, in the arsenal, General Douglas MacArthur was born in 1880. His father, Captain Arthur MacArthur and Mrs. MacArthur came to the arsenal as commandant during the Reconstruction Period after the Civil War. There are a couple of interesting places in the park. First is the Arkansas Arts Center which features changing exhibits, a gift shop, and a little restaurant called the Vineyard in the Park, a project of the Fine Arts Club, the center's volunteer organization. The art center is open 10:00 A.M. to 5:00 P.M. Monday through Saturday and noon to 5:00 P.M. on Sunday and lunch is served from 11:30 A.M. to 1:30 P.M. Monday through Friday. Call (501) 372–4000.

Second is the Museum of Science and History on East 9th Street. It is the only remaining structure of the original arsenal. Birders will enjoy Ornithology Hall, and others will be fascinated by the Nature Gallery, which shows the geology, weather, and land formations of Arkansas. The museum is open year-round Monday through Saturday from 9:00 A.M. to 4:30 P.M., Sunday from 1:00 to 4:00 P.M. Call (501) 371–3521.

The Arkansas Art Center's Decorative Arts Museum, housed in the Pike-Fletcher-Terry Mansion at Seventh and Rock streets in the

Quarter, is a 3-story beauty full of mirrors, crystal, silver services, and carved wooden decorative items used in homes over the years. The museum has both permanent collections and changing exhibits. The Crystal Room is a mirrored area filled with crystal on glass displays, almost resulting in a fun-house effect. Each room has its own fireplace. In 1839 the original house—a seven-room brick home—was built on grounds large enough to make it self-sufficient, including slave quarters, a smokehouse, and a detached kitchen. It was occupied by federal troops during the Civil War. In 1916 it was remodeled into its present Colonial Revival style, complete with a lead glass skylight opened by a pulley in the attic. The museum is open weekdays from 10:00 A.M. to 5:00 P.M. and Sunday from noon to 5:00 P.M. Call (501) 374–9479.

Enough tourist stuff—let's get serious and talk about food. Better yet, let's stop talking and find **Andre's** in Hillcrest, a restaurant owned by Swiss pastry chef Andre Simon. The establishment is at 605 North Beechwood, in a small house painted a bright robin's egg blue. A sign in the yard has the Swiss flag logo on it. (You might miss it if you're not looking for it.) Most of the interior walls have been removed, and exposed beams give the place an informal feel. The menu, written on a large chalkboard on an easel, lists about ten entrees available. A grill cook can be seen at work in the far corner. Items as varied as pasta, seafood, beef, and chicken range in price from $8.50 to $16.95. There are soups and salads, and the entrees are accompanied by generous portions of potatoes and vegetables. The small wine list of carefully selected wines, both imported and domestic, is quite good, and the weekend brunch is popular. And, of course, breads and pastries are on display to tempt you into the original sin—eating forbidden stuff. The restaurant is open from 11:00 A.M. to 2:00 P.M. (from 10:00 A.M. to 2:00 P.M. on Sunday) and from 6:00 to 9:30 P.M. seven days a week. Call (501) 666–9191 for reservations.

Cantrell Gallery, at 8206 Cantrell Road, has more than 3,500 square feet of gallery area featuring an eclectic group of art from local artists around the state. But what makes this gallery different is its permanent display of abstract art by Mary the Asian elephant (more about her later). Gallery owner Helen Scott has about twenty-five of Mary's paintings on exhibit, for sale, in the front gallery. Mary's oils sell from $100 to $350. The gallery is open from 10:00 A.M. to 5:30 P.M. Monday through Saturday; call (501) 224–1335.

With Little Rock as the hub, explore some surrounding towns. I–40 northwest leads to Maumelle, site of the Central Arkansas Hot Air Balloon Port. Maumelle is also where **Ron Mynatt's Woodcarvings** of faces and realistic busts in various types of wood are carved. Ron enjoys talking about the "spirit faces" he carves. The idea was imported from the Black Forest of Germany, where faces were carved on trees to protect the forest from fire and flood. When houses were built, wood-carvers came and carved a face on the main ceiling beam in the hope of uncovering a benevolent spirit to protect the home from fire and flood—"sort of an early homeowners' policy," notes Ron, who started carving wood in college and has been doing it ever since. Ron's walking sticks vary from the smallest (2-inch face) for $25 to the larger ones for $45. Some of the largest carvings he does are on cypress knees that stand about 4 feet tall and have 24-inch faces on them. The more detailed western series of hard-faced (excuse the pun) gamblers, trappers, Indians, and mountaineers with hats and vests in incredible detail are about $150. Ron works in his garage, where he displays his finished carvings. To find him, take the Maumelle/Morgan exit from I–40 and then call him at (501) 851–7279. He is home evenings and weekends.

Here is a special note for serious hikers: the **Ouachita Trail** begins at Pinnacle Mountain State Park, just across the Arkansas River from Maumelle on Highway 30. The mountain rises more than a thousand feet into the sky above the Arkansas River Valley, a wedge of rock jutting abruptly from the flat valley. Surrounded by heavily wooded hillsides, bright waterways and rich lowlands, the summit offers a panoramic view of the eastern slopes of the Ouachita Mountain range. There are hiking trails for everyone in this day-use park, from the gentle half-mile loop for the physically limited to the day trip for birders and wildflower hunters, to the infamous Ouachita Trail that extends more than 250 miles into eastern Oklahoma for serious, really serious, hikers. The starting point of this awesome trail is just west of the Visitors' Center and is marked with blue blazes. So, if you are headed for Oklahoma, and not in a hurry, call (501) 868–9150 for trail information.

Driving north on I–40 from Little Rock, you'll find the city of Conway between the towns of Pickles Gap and Toad Suck. Conway has a nice downtown area full of shops, all neatly topped with awnings. Probably the most interesting new place in town is **Pastimes Restaurant,** at 713 Oak Street, owned by David and

Carol Darnell. Connoisseur's Collection, an antiques mall, and a "previously owned" designer clothing shop are there as well. People come in to stroll around and shop, not just to eat. The boutique of previously owned designer clothing shares the front half of the building with the restaurant, while the back half comprises 15,000 square feet of antique furniture. The mood of the restaurant is elegant in the tree-filled, green, and open spaces. Classical music plays softly, mirrors and trellises separate the dining areas, and antique sideboards and hall trees line the room. The lunch menu has sandwiches as unusual as a Reuben inside a French puff pastry shell or a Cajun poor boy.

The Darnells cook everything. David—who has worked under chefs in several cities—does the French-influenced entrees, (seafood lasagna with lobster sauce), traditional southern dishes, and some French-Cajun specialties. Carol makes the breads and luscious desserts, such as fresh Key Lime Pie or the Banana Flip (puff pastry with fresh bananas and a Bavarian créme sauce). Now that they are open for breakfast, you can enjoy a monster (8-inch) homemade cinnamon roll with David's freshly ground gourmet coffee. Since this is a dry county, there is no wine list, but you can bring a bottle of wine and the waiter will open it for you. Entrees range from $7.95 to $14.99. To reach Pastimes, take exit 127 off I–40 and go south on Highway 64, which is Oak Street. Hours are Tuesday through Saturday from 8:00 A.M. to 9:00 P.M.; call (501) 327–2185.

Wooster, north on Highway 25 from Conway, is a good place for a romantic getaway from the city in an elegant old Victorian. The **Patton House Inn,** at 14 Reed Road (Highway 25), was built in 1918. The house is surrounded by old shade trees and is near Beaverfork Lake; plenty of antiques and crafts shops are in the area, too. The inn's proprietor, Mary Lee Patton Shirley, is the niece of the original owners of the two-story home. Two bedrooms on the second floor share a bath; one bedroom has a queen-size bed and a balcony overlooking the six-and-a-half-acre yard; and there is one bedroom with a private bath downstairs. Room prices are $50, which includes a breakfast of sausage soufflé, French toast sticks with syrup, toasted English muffins, fresh fruit, juice, and coffee. Mary Lee says you probably won't want lunch—how's that for understatement? Call (501) 679–2975 for reservations.

Riddle: What does someone do with a baby elephant when it reaches 6,000 pounds? The answer is a Riddle, too—Scott Riddle, to be exact. **Riddle's Elephant Breeding Farm and**

Wildlife Sanctuary is where Scott Riddle and his wife, Heidi, care for elephants from all over the world, elephants no longer wanted by the places that were once their homes. Elephants too old, too cranky, or injured in some way are routinely destroyed every year. Because they are almost extinct, because there are so few places left to support elephants in their natural environment, and because the Riddles wanted to do something for this endangered animal, the couple bought 330 acres off Pumpkin Center Circle between Guy and Quitman (on Highway 25) and took them in. The farm contains a spring-fed creek, a waterfall, a pasture, and forestland. The Riddles have recently completed a 2,000-yard swimming hole for their eight jumbo guests.

Two such guests are Solomon and Mugsy (called "the little guys"), seven-year-old African elephants that were to be killed in a culling, or herd-thinning operation, in their native land. A wealthy man who bought them as calves and then watched them grow to 6,000 pounds soon tired of caring for them (a full-grown male can weigh six tons and stand 12 feet tall). African elephant Willie (from the Nashville Zoo, hence his name) joined Toby, a twelve-year-old male, and Tonga, a fourteen-year-old female from a small Indiana zoo. Asian elephants Kate and Betty Boop came from a circus, where they were injured by an overwrought male (females weigh only half as much as males and are shorter by 4 feet; they are no match in a domestic dispute).

Scott Riddle's most famous elephant is Mary, a seventeen-year-old Asian elephant with an artistic bent. Her paintings hang in the Cantrell Gallery in Little Rock (see page 141), where they bring as much as $350. (Asian elephants, a separate species, are smaller—if you can call it that—and often lack tusks.) Riddle, who is also an artist, calls Mary's style "impressionist"; Helen Scott of the gallery sees it as "abstract." But whether in the style of Monet or Picasso, Mary likes primary colors, "with red her favorite," Riddle says. Mary's talents don't stop there. She also plays the drum, the bell, the tambourine, and, believe it or not, the harmonica. She travels to Pickles Gap with "the little guys" for $3.00 elephant rides and does her share to support her $100.00-a-week food habit. Mary is the primary fund-raiser. In the wild elephants eat 500 to 600 pounds of food a day—that's a lot of groceries—and even with high-nutrition elephant chow, 100 pounds a day is average. The nonprofit operation is constantly searching for ways to bring in funds.

"Mary" at Riddle's Elephant Breeding Farm and Wildlife Sanctuary

The Riddles are even active on the world scene. In 1991 the nation of Zimbabwe began destroying elephants, and the Riddles sent protests through their congressman to try to stop the killing. "We would take them all if we could find the money to move them," Scott says. Long-range plans include massive, pachyderm-size barns; medical facilities; and the corralling of a large pasture to allow all the elephants to roam unchained, as Boop and Kate do now. Scott also wants to open an elephant museum with his collection of more than 1,500 elephant items—ancient temple rubbings, figurines, and prints—and large assortment of books on the subject.

The farm is home to a collection of geese, goats, dogs, cats, and chickens right now, but the designation "wildlife sanctuary" entitles the Riddles to take in any zoo or circus animal that might otherwise be destroyed. Most funding comes from individual memberships ($25) and corporate sponsorship of the farm. "This is not a job; it's a life," Riddle says. Call (501) 589–3291 for directions to the farm and a chance to hear the incredible vocabulary of sounds these gentle creatures use to communicate—25 different sounds, ranging from high-frequency whistles to deep rumbles, two octaves below human range—and an unbeatable photo opportunity.

Traveling north on Highway 5 from I–30 north of Little Rock will lead to Romance, guaranteed. Louise Berry, post office clerk in Romance, spends all day on Valentine's Day stamping postmarks on love letters from across the country.

If you have found Romance, John and Susan Hammon's nearby 110-acre Brahman cattle farm, **Hammons Chapel Farm,** at 271 Hammons Chapel Road (1 mile off Highway 5), might be just the place to stop. It's north of Romance on Highway 5. This single-story stucco house with its red tile roof is very open and modern. It has only one room for guests; it's a true bed-and-breakfast in the European style. The guest room, with twin beds and private bath, is fine for a quiet visit, or you can help with the farm chores. Susan says, "We can use all the help we can get." They try to make people feel at home, she says, and tells the story of the honeymoon couple who helped load a bull into the trailer and then showed up at the state fair to help unload it. The $45 price includes a breakfast geared to the guests' preference, and Susan says she will gladly offer dinner as well, since the farm is "out in the country." She will even fix a picnic lunch for a trip to Greers Ferry Lake or the Ozark Folk Center. Call (501) 849–2819 for reservations.

Not far from Little Rock, thanks to I–40, is the town of Brinkley. There the **Great Southern Hotel,** at 127 West Cedar Street, is a restored railroad hotel complete with antique bathtubs and furnishings dating from 1915. Innkeepers Stanley and Dorcas Prince have turned it into not only a bed-and-breakfast but a popular tearoom that also serves lunch and dinner southern-style. The humongous pink marble lobby, in a sea of mosaic tile, and the 15-

foot pressed tin ceilings reflect the feeling of the original sixty-one-room hotel; today only four rooms, with private baths, are available—all on the first floor. Most of the attention is given to the restaurant, which is filled with white-lace-over-peach-covered tables and crystal goblets. A 1914 Model T vegetable huckster's truck serves as a buffet. The big windows with peach curtains and a high tin ceiling with fans give the room a light and airy feel. More acres of mosaic tile cover the floor here, too. Massive brick pillars—a dozen of them—and a porch surround the hotel.

Regional southern cooking features such entrees as Mississippi Flyway Duck, grilled and stuffed with onions and apples and served with Bigarade Sauce, or Pecan Fried Chicken, a boneless breast of chicken dipped in an egg batter with toasted pecans, deep-fried, and served with milk gravy. The menu changes from day to day and ranges from lamb chops to seafood. A specialty is Arkansas rice, which joins vegetables, soup, and salad bar, and a full table of desserts. Guests of the B & B enjoy a continental breakfast served in their rooms, which are priced at $44. Restaurant hours are from 11:00 A.M. to 2:00 P.M. for lunch and from 5:00 to 9:00 P.M. for dinner, Monday through Saturday. Call (501) 734-4955 for reservations.

An impressive archaeological site, even though misnamed, **Toltec Mounds** lie southwest of Little Rock off Highway 165. An early owner thought these were the mounds of the Toltec Indians of Mexico, but the people who built the mounds and lived in the central part of the state had a culture different from that of other contemporary groups in the Mississippi Valley. They were not nomads but lived in permanent villages where they built sturdy houses and farmed the rich soil. For more than twelve years now, the Arkansas Archaeological Survey and volunteers from the Arkansas Archaeological Society have been digging for answers about the lives of a culture named Plum Bayou who lived here about A.D. 700 to 950. Guides take visitors through areas of the central plaza and five of the original eighteen mounds. The nearby Arkansas River was used for transportation and fishing, and clay was used for pottery; the soil was fertile, and the surrounding uplands supported an abundance of animals for hunting. A dugout canoe measuring 24 feet was found in the Saline River, miraculously preserved, perhaps because of being quickly buried in mud. This and other artifacts are on display at the park. In June you can watch digs under way by the Arkansas Archaeological Survey. The mounds are on Highway 386, 9 miles north-west of the town of England, off Highway 165. The park is open Tuesday through Saturday from 8:00 A.M. to 5:00 P.M. and Sunday from noon to 5:00 P.M. Call (501) 961–9442.

Sixteen miles southeast of Little Rock on old Highway 165, which parallels I–40, is **Marlsgate Plantation,** a working plantation with 2,000 acres of cotton and a beautiful, thirty-three room mansion on Bearskin Lake, an oxbow lake, in the center of it. This wooded setting is where David Garner and his grandmother, Grace Cupit Newman, live. The plantation, a lovingly maintained beauty, is a picture of Victorian elegance, and the ties between Arkansas and the Deep South are plain to see. David serves lunches to groups of sixteen or more and has an antiques, flower, and gift shop in the carriage house. The mansion is 5 miles off the road and not visible from the highway, but tours of this private home can be arranged on an individual basis by appointment; call (501) 961–1307.

Just across the river from Little Rock in North Little Rock, *The Spirit,* Arkansas Riverboat Company's beautiful white and red paddlewheel riverboat, still plies the river as riverboats have done for more than 150 years. The journey used to be a perilous adventure, dodging sandbars and logjams; now it's just fun. The excursions departing from North Little Rock for one-, two-, and three-hour cruises from May through September feature Dixieland music, dinner-dance cruises, and moonlight dance cruises; also offered are one-hour daytime cruises by grassy Riverfront Park under the city skyline, during which the pilot describes the history of the changing shoreline and points out the rock bluff landmark that gave the city its name. The riverboat has full bar service. Call (501) 376–4150 for a current schedule.

Index

Index

Index

Japanese-American Relocation Center, 123
Jasper, 42
Jessieville, 86
Jimmy Driftwood Barn, 8
Jimmy Lile's Knives, 74
Johnson House Bed & Breakfast, 57
Jonesboro, 30
Ka-Do-Ha Indian Village, 104
Kingston, 45
Klappenbach Bakery, 134
La Bella Gourmet Gifts and Delicatessen, 118
Lake Catherine State Park, 97
Lake Chicot, 123
Lake Village, 123
Lakeview, 19
Langley, 105
Lepanto, 27
Leslie, 39
Levi Wilcoxon Demonstration Forest, 122
Lithia Springs Bed and Breakfast Lodge, 15
Little Missouri Falls, 106
Little Rock, 138
Logoly State Park, 115
Lois Gean's, 116
Louisiana Purchase Historic Marker, 125
Lum and Abner Museum, 109
MacArthur Park, 140
Magnolia, 115
Malvern, 96
Mammoth Springs, 21
Margland II, 132
Marlsgate Plantation, 148
Mary Maestri's, 56
Mary Woods Number 2 Steamboat, 3
Maumelle, 142
Maxine's International Coffee House, 90
Maynard, 25
Maynard Pioneer Museum, 25
McClard's, 90
McCollum-Chidester House, 112
McGehee, 123
McNeil, 115
McSpadden's Dulcimer Shop, 7

Index

Index

About the Author

Patti DeLano is a free-lance travel writer and photographer who has lived in the Ozarks of Missouri and vacationed across the border in Arkansas for the past twenty years. She and her husband, Bob, were crewmembers for Trans World Airline and, since retirement, now travel extensively. Patti has paddled canoes and landed trout; she and Bob refurbished a Victorian house and filled it with antiques; Bob is a golfer and racing enthusiast; and they both enjoy good restaurants and fine wines. All these interests are reflected in Patti's books, which include *Missouri: Off the Beaten Path* and *Kansas: Off the Beaten Path*, written with coauthor and illustrator Cathy Johnson. The DeLanos' youngest son, Chris, is a student at a Missouri university.

About the Illustrator

Cathy Johnson, naturalist, artist, and writer, has illustrated three Off the Beaten Path books and coauthored two. With twelve books to her credit, Cathy and her husband, Harris, live in Excelsior Springs, Missouri, where she has a studio in the woods.